NOT JUST TALKING

Help your child communicate — from day one

NOT JUST TALKING

Help your child communicate – from day one

Sioban Boyce

CONTENTS

INTRODUCTION

WHAT IS A CONVERSATION 6

Conversation is not just talking 6
About this book   7
'It can't be my child's problem' 8

PART ONE

IS IT REALLY NOT JUST
TALKING?   12

So what part do conversations
    play in our lives?   12
Where do conversations
    happen?   12
How conversations work   13
What has changed?   14
What part does language
    play?   17

INTERPRETATIONAL SKILLS 18

What exactly is body
    language?   18
What do situations tell us?   21

CONVERSATIONAL SKILLS 21

What does a listener need
    to do?   24
What does a speaker need
    to do?   25
Additional skills   25
Prosody   26
What about 'eye contact'?   27
And finally ...   27

PART TWO

A MODERN MALADY   30

How do babies learn non-verbal
communication skills? • The first
few hours • The way we talk to
our babies • Family life • Shopping
habits • Television — a new
perspective • As your child grows

THE FIRST 24 HOURS   32

A fascination for faces — how it
all begins • The moment of birth
• Why are faces important?
• How to encourage facial interest

SIGN TO YOUR BABY   34

Your baby learns to understand
signs • How does signing help
my baby understand what I am
saying? • Teaching your baby
• Some signs to try

WHAT IS YOUR BABY
TRYING TO SAY?   36

The first attempt at communication
• Distinguish his different cries
• Listen and wait • Notice what
he looks at • As baby starts to
move about

STRUCTURE AND ROUTINE 38

Help baby make sense of her
daily routine • Making sense of
her day • What is she trying to
tell you? • Start and finish • Still
unsettled? • Cranial osteopathy
• Time for Mum • Developing
an interest in routine

GIVE AND TAKE   41

The two-way process of
conversations • The art of
conversation • The early days
of interacting • Taking it further

ONE THING LEADS TO
ANOTHER   42

The learning curve • Teaching
your baby to predict • Nursery
rhymes • How to enhance
prediction skills

MAKING SENSE OF IT ALL 44

Developing non-verbal
understanding • Facial
expressions again! • Modelling
behaviour • Keep language
simple and clear
• Understanding situations

BABY EQUIPMENT   46

How equipment can help or
hinder communication • Can
your baby can see people
holding conversations? • The
buggy (and any equipment that
keeps your baby at knee height)
• Car seats

KNOWING ME,
KNOWING YOU   48

Becoming self-aware • Recognising
himself and others • Introduce
mirrors and photos • How to
extend mirror play • You and
me • Moving away from others
• Making people laugh
• Something more you can do

ALL THE RIGHT
INGREDIENTS   51

What makes nursery rhymes so
important? • Look at me! What
am I doing? • Encouraging
expectation and prediction
• Developing intonation
patterns, stress and rhythm
• Becoming a good speaker
and listener

EARLY USE OF NON-VERBAL
SKILLS   53

Exploring touch, gesture,
voice and facial expression
• Touchy-feely • Encourage
the use of gestures • How does
your baby's voice develop?
• Helping your baby babble
• Encourage facial expressions
• A game to encourage touch
and gesture

EATING TOGETHER   55

Why family mealtimes are so
important • How can spoon
feeding help conversational
development? • How does the
family meal table help?
• Signal the beginnings and
endings of activities • Help
your baby develop different
conversational styles

COPING WITH CHANGE   57

Some complex skills that
your baby needs to master
• Encourage your baby to imitate
others • Now focus on choosing

• Why is change so important? •
How to tackle change • Leading
actions and games

YOUR BABY STARTS
SIGNING TOO   59

Now she can tell people what
she wants • Skills your baby must
have • How will your baby learn
to make the signs? • Does signing
teach your baby other skills?

GETTING READY TO TALK   61

How to prepare for speaking
• The crying • The cooing and
babbling • Put a name to
everything • When the words
start coming

HOW TO TALK TO YOUR
BABY   63

Keep things clear and simple
• Should I talk in full sentences?
• Don't ask questions when there
isn't a genuine choice • The use
of 'please' and 'thank you'
• Combining words and signs
• React to actions and events

PART THREE
FROM TALKING TO
SCHOOL ENTRY   66

A great leap forward • The
essential conversational skills

NOW LOOK WHO'S
TALKING!   68

Her first words • Signing to talking
• Can you understand her?

WHAT DOES THAT MEAN?   70
Get ready, get set   70
Body language and facial
   expressions   71
How will your child learn to
   use body language?   75
Touch   77
Proximity and personal space   78
Making sense of situations   79
Making connections   80
Hidden meanings   81

KNOWING WHAT
YOU FEEL   84
What do Mummy and Daddy
   feel?   84
How to help her   85
Complex interpretation   85
Which emotions should I show
   her?   86
She has feelings too   87
Different levels of emotional
   understanding   87
How to identify feelings in
   others   88

WHO AM I?   90
Self-awareness   90
Interest in others   91
Understanding family
   relationships   93
Friends and strangers   93
Shared knowledge   93

MAKING CONVERSATIONS
WORK   96
Being a good listener   97
What a speaker needs
   to do   100
The sound of her voice   107
Taking turns   107
Sharing information   109
Can she talk in group
   situations?   110
Can she negotiate?   110

WHAT TO TALK ABOUT   112
Can he request
   information?   112
Making a reply   114
The use of 'please'   114
Asking for help   115
Language styles   115

MAKING AND KEEPING
FRIENDS   117
Starting friendships   117
How to help your child make
   friends   118
The difference between
   making and keeping
   friends   118
Will she be able to make
   friends on her own?   119

Building friendships   120
Dealing with conflict   120

RELATED SKILLS   121
Symbolic understanding   121
Start and finish   122
Prediction   123
The importance of
   experience   126
What is choice?   126
Dealing with change   128
'Rules'   129
Connecting and
   generalisation   130
Speculation   131
Fantasy versus reality   132

TROUBLESOME CHILDREN 134
Use of pictures, symbols
   and signs   134
How to talk to your child   136
Information-carrying words   136
How best to praise her   136
Information giving   136
Using books to promote
   conversational skills   138
What to avoid   139

WHAT SHOULD I LOOK
OUT FOR?   140
Signs that he might be
   struggling   140
Be aware   141
Tantrums   142
Stranger danger   145
Children with more complex
   needs   145

WHAT HAPPENS ON
SCHOOL ENTRY?   147
Primary school   147
Entry to class – first day   148

CONCLUSION   150

References and further
   reading   150

INTRODUCTION

WHAT IS A CONVERSATION?

Any conversation must have three elements: speaker, message, listener. Each element needs to function effectively for the conversation to be successful.

Day in, day out we rely on successful conversation. Every interaction or exchange that we have — at the bus stop, in the shops, at school or work, with family, friends, teachers, colleagues or strangers — depends to some degree on communicating successfully through conversation.

CONVERSATION IS NOT JUST TALKING

The development of communication is an amazing process. Every parent longs to hear their child talking. However, talking may not signal the start of communication. Sixty to 90 per cent of any conversation is non-verbal, that is, the message is communicated through something other than words — gesture, body language, intonation, clues from the situation, past experience and so on.

In order for us to communicate well our brains must rapidly compute all kinds of information in addition to the words spoken or heard. It is this non-verbal information that enables us to understand:

- what to say
- when to say it
- whether to say it
- how to say it.

Non-verbal skills are the bedrock of your child's ability to communicate effectively. Without them, she will learn how to use grammar and articulation, and will even develop a wide vocabulary, but she will not know how to hold a conversation, how to give the right information and how to respond to the feelings and needs of other people.

Children who cannot effectively process non-verbal information are at a severe disadvantage. They may be very good talkers but they will be unable to communicate successfully because they will miss out on vital clues that help them have satisfactory conversational exchanges. They will find it difficult to make sense of what is happening around them or convey what they want.

As a result these children may resort to undesirable behaviours — fits of anger, withdrawal, hitting out — as a way of venting their frustration. This in turn can lead to serious difficulties at home and in school, reducing your child's ability

to make friends, achieve her potential at school or enjoy family life to the full.

But help is at hand. You can learn to give your baby the best start in life by supporting the development of her non-verbal skills — from day one. And if you are the parents of an older child who may be showing signs of problems arising from poor non-verbal understanding, you can improve her life forever by introducing the simple techniques explained in this book.

ABOUT THIS BOOK

Not Just Talking: Help your child communicate — from day one is about non-verbal skills and the problems associated with failure to develop them. It also has practical ideas for you to use to develop the missing skills in your child. Throughout the book there are 'Focus points' and suggestions to help you promote the skills described. These activities can be expanded and developed in pre-school settings for use with all children to ensure they have adequate communication skills — a high priority target for governments.

When I trained as a speech and language therapist during the 1970s, the focus of our training was the verbal skills — articulation, vocabulary and grammar — and little

mention was made of the 60–90 per cent of communication that is non-verbal. In the 1980s it became apparent that many children could talk well but were showing signs of difficulty in making friends, behaving as expected, benefiting from education and communicating about their emotions. It became apparent to me that a lack of non-verbal understanding and skill was at the root of this problem.

For 20 years I have specialised in the development of non-verbal communication skills — how you learn to read and use facial expressions and body language, how you interpret situations and, then, how you relate all this information to previous experiences in order to communicate successfully. I have helped hundreds of children of all ages — including many diagnosed as having Asperger's Syndrome or as being on the autistic spectrum — to become competent, sociable and effective communicators, to shine as individuals. Now I want to share my knowledge with every parent.

Books for parents on the development of communication focus almost entirely on aspects of spoken language. *Not Just Talking: Help your child communicate — from day one* is different because it shows you how your child learns to understand body

language and other important non-verbal clues necessary for good communication. It covers the period from birth until your child starts school. It contains everything you need to promote your child's conversational skills.

PART ONE

Part One explains what non-verbal communication is and how to recognise these skills in your child. This will help you promote your child's ability to hold good conversations. If she simply learns to use her language skills and doesn't acquire non-verbal understanding she will not know how to hold a conversation and will find daily living difficult.

PART TWO

Part Two covers the period from birth until your child begins to talk, and is in a style that will be easy to use when you are dealing with the arrival of your new baby. It is written in 'bite-sized' chunks so you can pick it up, read a paragraph and get practical ideas you can try out immediately.

PART THREE

Part Three relates to the period before your child goes to school. It goes into more detail and contains a bit more background to help you fully understand the importance of your child developing all these essential skills — and what might happen if she doesn't.

This book is written primarily for parents but is also essential reading for anyone who works with children — particularly those in pre-school settings, as well as midwives, health visitors and social workers. Professionals will be able to use the book as a companion and checklist for ensuring that children on their caseloads are able to use all the recommended skills.

With older children who have not developed the non-verbal skills described, the book can be used to help identify the skills they lack. With good non-verbal ability, your child will be better able to benefit fully from her education.

'IT CAN'T BE MY CHILD'S PROBLEM'

Our way of living has changed so much in the last 30 years or so that children do not spend sufficient time observing how people communicate and interact with each other. Nor do they participate as often in household activities and other aspects of daily living as previous generations did.

You will see how the changing pattern of family meals and the introduction of personal screens (TV, laptops, mobile

phones) have had a severe impact on the development of non-verbal communication. As you read this book, always keep in mind that children have to watch, think about, store and then practise the skills they observe. If this doesn't happen, your child can't learn to understand what all this non-verbal information means and how it affects what we say and do.

My experience has shown me that children who struggle with any communication difficulty find their lives very hard and may make life very difficult for their families. Without the ability to process non-verbal information, we may as well be living on another planet. Children who fail to develop sufficient skills in effect do just that — they opt out of conversations by connecting instead with TV, computer or texts and isolate themselves or become withdrawn.

If you make sure that your child is able to use all the skills suggested then family life should run relatively smoothly. Bringing up children has its challenges, but if your child can communicate well, those times will be less stressful for all the family.

If your child is showing signs of any problems in communication, socialisation, emotional development or behaviour, this book can help you. Even slight problems while she is small may grow to become more serious difficulties by the time she reaches secondary school. So the earlier you can help her the better.

It is important to understand that problems with non-verbal skills have no bearing on your child's intelligence level. Many of the children I work with are highly intelligent, but because their conversational skills are poor they are not able to take advantage of learning situations. However, as their non-verbal communication skills develop through the Not Just Talking intervention programme, they very quickly become able to learn at school and their educational progress noticeably improves.

Conversational skills are also at the heart of being able to make and keep friends, which helps us develop positive relationships. With well-developed non-verbal skills we have a good sense of what others feel and we can recognise and name our own feelings. Everything we do every day is dependent on how we process the non-verbal clues available to us.

You can easily develop these skills in your child and it makes really good sense to do so. Your child can be a confident and capable communicator.

PART ONE

IS IT REALLY NOT JUST TALKING?

In this part of the book I will go through key non-verbal skill areas and will explain their function within a conversation so that you know what skills your child needs to have for good communication. Part Two and Part Three focus on babies and toddlers, putting these skills into context and giving you simple ideas for encouraging their development and use.

On the following pages you will see that the give-and-take nature of a conversation is underpinned by an understanding of many aspects of non-verbal communication. To be entirely clear, this book is not concerned with understanding high-level, subtly nuanced skills used in adult life — the slight tilt of the body that indicates interest in the opposite sex or a touch to the head as a subconscious indication of an apology, for instance. These skills are only learned later in life, as a teenager, and when all the skills spoken about here are in place.

SO WHAT PART DO CONVERSATIONS PLAY IN OUR LIVES?

Conversations are central to the way we live our lives; we share information with others all day long and if your child is unable to do so effectively it may well impact on some or all of the following areas of his life:

- how he learns to understand emotions and then how to express those emotions
- how he communicates his ideas to others
- how confident he becomes and his level of self-esteem

Friends playing
These girls are playing 'dressing up'. There will be lots to talk about and having shared this game they can refer back to it on another day.

- how he makes friends and then develops those friendships into meaningful relationships
- how he plays with other children
- how he behaves in different areas of his daily life — home, playgroup, out shopping and so on
- how he copes at school, and how this influences the way his work life progresses.

A child who lacks essential non-verbal conversational skills will be lost and confused, and will have low levels of confidence. This will lead to him having poor self-esteem and few, if any, friends. Here you will see what happens when children are unable to participate in conversations from a position of strength and how they will resort to other less socially acceptable methods of communication.

WHERE DO CONVERSATIONS HAPPEN?
Conversations happen one-to-one, in small or large groups, on the phone and when sending emails or texts or any other written method of communication. For the purpose of this book, however, I will focus on the development of all aspects of spoken conversation. Without a firm grounding in non-verbal conversational skills, your

child will not go on to develop the communication skills required for reading and writing.

As you may well have experienced yourself, conversations that involve more than two people are much more difficult than one-to-one. In a conversation between two people, you only have to concentrate on one other person's non-verbal communication. With just one additional person participating, the conversation demands a higher level of skill and experience.

Talking on the phone is even harder because you cannot see the person you are speaking to. You have to pay special attention to subtle non-verbal clues, such as tone of voice or the stress on certain words, to know which words you should listen to and which you can ignore. Your child will only develop this level of understanding if he has already picked up the more basic signals and signs.

When a young child enters school, he also needs the ability to detect the complex signals from large groups, such as school assembly. Suddenly all the non-verbal skills he has developed up to this point become very useful. Once he has experienced assembly and the playground a few times, he should start to recognise the clues that help him fully understand meaning, so that he knows how to behave and what to say or not say. If your child has not developed these skills, his understanding of what he should do or say will be undermined and his communication level may revert to that of a much younger child.

Adults holding a conversation
These children are going round a park in a group with a guide. Adults are asking and replying to questions, modelling good conversational skills to the children.

There are many other stressful situations where, even when we are adult, our communicative ability deteriorates; adults can have tantrums just like children, usually under extreme circumstances. Being older, however, we have developed more skills and experience, and are better able to cope with stress. Stress has less impact on adults than on children, who are still acquiring skills.

HOW CONVERSATIONS WORK
These are the key features of all conversations:

1. Information (the message) passes between two or more people; it is a two-way process.

2. A conversation only works when there is a sender (speaker), a receiver (listener) and a meaningful message that suits the needs of both parties.

3. The listener always needs to give feedback. The listener might appear not to be participating in the conversation, but feedback demonstrates they are interested and/or understand what is said to them — or perhaps that they need more or less information. Often this feedback is given non-verbally, ie there may be no spoken response. Without this feedback from the listener you do not have a conversation and therefore the message will not be transmitted effectively. This is every bit as important when addressing a large group as when talking person-to-person.

4. All three elements of the conversation — the speaker, the listener, the message — have to be valued by all participating in the conversation and need to work equally well. It is no good if the speaker dominates the conversation without any reference to how the listener receives the message or if the message is in a language not understood by the listener.

Later we will look in detail at which non-verbal communication skills are involved — remember they make up 60–90 per cent of the message (see page 6). First, however, it is important to understand why children may have difficulty acquiring them.

WHAT HAS CHANGED?
A baby or child only picks up non-verbal communication skills through the daily experience of watching both sides of a conversation. There

have been many social and technological changes that prevent children from doing this and have a detrimental impact on their ability to make sense of people's feelings and thoughts.

Think of the changes in the way we live our lives. For instance, in the past people used to eat round a table at home, at school or in the workplace, three times a day, and without a TV in the room. Now it might only happen once a week and/or people focus on what the TV is saying. Nowadays, too, children no longer play in the street with friends, and play tends to be in the home and may be around a computer screen.

Changes such as these occurred without anyone realising the impact on children's development of non-verbal understanding. It is not the fault of parents if these changes affect children's communicative ability; they are simply part of our changing social pattern. As a society, we just need to learn to adapt our behaviour a little to ensure all children grow up able to communicate effectively.

Children playing outside
These children are having such a good time that others might want to join in. There will be plenty of opportunities to practise conversations.

HOW DOES THE FAMILY MEAL TABLE HELP?

The meal table is an excellent place for children to learn many non-verbal communication skills. These include:

Prediction

- Your child will see the table being laid and the process of the meal being served, each step in the sequence having a beginning and an end.
- Noticing the beginnings and ends of activities, with obvious signs for these activities, is easy at the meal table. Later your child will need to develop this recognition to the much more subtle level of identifying the beginning and endings of words and phrases.
- From seeing the end of each part of the process he will learn to predict what is coming next.

Non-verbal interpretation

- Your child will see how other people interact as they prepare the meal, join the table and so on.
- Watching the family talking, he will see the body language and facial expressions that indicate concentration, frustration, excitement etc.
- Your child will learn to draw conclusions from information he sees. For example, he sees his daddy get the bib and plate, which means it is nearly time to have some food. He might show signs of anticipation.

Speaker and listener roles

- Your child will see people initiating conversations, looking at each other and giving feedback.

Styles of talking

- At the meal table, your child will hear people asking questions, making jokes, requesting help, giving information, telling stories.

However, none of this will be possible if you have a TV present in the kitchen and your family are watching it, because you will be modelling to your child that you can look at the TV, eat and talk at the same time. This is OK for experienced communicators, but not for children who are learning how to interpret information.

THE IMPACT OF SCREENS

Think how the screen has begun to dominate all aspects of our lives. Only a few decades ago children spent a very small amount of time in front of a screen, but today there is a tendency for them to spend many hours a day watching TV or using mobile phones or computers of various sorts. There

HIGHWAY CODE

Over the last 40 years I have come to realise that in order to utter his first word a child needs to have attained a certain level of competence in non-verbal communication. Older children who are unable to talk will start to do so only when the non-verbal skills are sufficiently developed.

Think of it like learning to drive a car. You can learn all the Highway Code and find out about what the accelerator and brake are for. You might even know how to get the car going and be able to drive the car, but if you can only drive up and down your road, it won't get you very far.

You need more complex driving skills – and experience – to help you drive in towns and on motorways, in the wet or at night. The more experience you have, the better you get. Learning to drive requires us to know about the rules of driving, the equipment we have and how to drive. The last of these only develops through practice and experience.

By developing your child's non-verbal skills, you are setting him on the road to life.

are now many children's television programmes, throughout the day, and there has been a massive rise in the number of home computers (children often have one in their bedroom), as well as a significant increase in gaming devices.

Children cannot learn non-verbal communication from TV and other screen-based technology. Sue Palmer, a consultant on the education of young children, long ago recognised the detrimental effect of screens and talks about it in detail in her *Toxic Childhood*. There is more on the impact of TV and computers later in this book.

Watching TV

These sisters are engrossed in watching TV and are missing opportunities to communicate with their parents or each other.

WHAT ABOUT THE BUGGY?

Parents may well do what all the books tell them to do, that is 'talk to your baby', but if the child is not facing them he will not benefit. In the first year or two, when his ability to understand words is developing fast but he is not yet competent, your child needs to be able to see people speaking to him and to one another in order to learn from observing the diversity of expressions, the glances, the shrugs and other nuances of non-verbal information. His language skills alone will not be sufficient to understand what is being said.

When buggies arrived on the scene in the early 1980s, with the obvious advantages of lightness of weight and ease of folding, we all thought that the baby or toddler would become more intelligent as a result of all the things that he could now see!

Chatting away
These parents are holding a wonderful conversation, but the poor little baby can see none of it!

Nobody thought about the fact that to make sense of this unfolding deluge of visual information he would need to develop some basic skills to know what to look at and what to ignore. See also pages 46–7.

WHAT PART DOES LANGUAGE PLAY?
A child may learn to talk well, with good articulation and grammar, but without non-verbal skills he will be unable to communicate well in a variety of day-to-day situations. Your child needs continuous experience if he is to understand the similarities and differences between situations and therefore know what to say and how to behave, in unfamiliar as well as familiar circumstances.

If his non-verbal skills are not sufficiently well developed when he starts talking, verbal language will take over and leave the non-verbal development behind. In this case he won't benefit from experience because he hasn't been used to looking at the signs that help him recognise the meaningful connections. So, for instance, he may be able to make sense of your facial expressions but be unable to generalise this to someone he has not seen before. His communicative ability will be very limited.

BUGGIES: A BABY'S VIEW

A significant point about the use of buggies or strollers rather than prams is that in a buggy the child may face away from whoever is pushing it.

Imagine a father wheeling his son in a buggy: the child is facing away from his father, so has no visual contact. When the dad speaks to the child, he won't know if his son is listening; and when he engages in conversation with another person, his child won't be watching all the non-verbal signals.

Also, a young child being pushed along with masses of visual information coming at high speed cannot process quickly what he is seeing. I recently saw a baby being pushed through a shopping centre in a buggy with five adults behind him talking animatedly. The baby became overwhelmed by the crowd and all the bustle. Because he couldn't see his parents, he was insecure, a look of terror came over him and he started to scream. The adults, unable to see his face, didn't understand why his behaviour had changed suddenly. If the baby had been looking at the adults, he would have been more secure in the knowledge that his parents were there. He would also have had the chance to watch and learn from the non-verbal interaction between the five people!

Think of it from the baby's perspective. He was looking outwards, away from the adults, and all that he could see was a new and confusing place that perhaps he had never been to before. He could hear in the distance the sound of his mother or father, whose voices he had only recently begun to recognise, but because he couldn't see them, he didn't feel safe.

INTERPRETATIONAL SKILLS

The first requirement for a successful conversation is to understand the topic, purpose and context in which it is taking place. On the basis of this we can predict what will happen next and have some idea about what others want to hear or say. So, correctly interpreting what is actually going on is a vital first step. The key elements your child needs to learn are associated with what bodies communicate and what situations tell us.

When acquiring all these skills your child must first learn the 'usual' clues. There are exceptions to any 'rule', but in order to understand these, it is essential that your child first learns to recognise the most common signs. She will learn that signs can communicate similar but different things. For instance, girls usually have longer hair than boys, but some girls have their hair cut shorter like a boy's haircut. Once she recognises the common connecting signs, learning the exceptions will be easy.

WHAT EXACTLY IS BODY LANGUAGE?
Body language to most people tends to mean facial expressions and gestures. But with regard to non-verbal understanding, body language is more comprehensive than this and includes all of the following:

1. Emotions — our bodies can communicate straightforward emotions. Think how different your body appears when cold, when you are laughing or jumping up and down with excitement or standing rigidly with fear.

2. Facial expressions — this includes those expressions that communicate emotions such as happiness, confusion, worry; the more subtle expressions such as attentiveness or disinterest; and indications of more nuanced messages such as sarcasm and innuendo.

3. Gestures — can be 'informal' automatic hand movements made alongside the spoken word, such as opening your hands out wide to communicate the size of the fish that got away!

GOOD PRACTICE

HSBC once ran a series of advertisements that demonstrated the fundamental importance of non-verbal communication, which the bank sees as central to good business practice. We saw that showing the soles of your feet is offensive to people in Thailand and a flat, palm-outward shove of the hand in Greece is seen as an insult. Yet neither of these gestures is problematic in the UK or the USA.

Gestures with a more definite meaning, as when waving goodbye or beckoning someone towards you — these are used in a more structured way and mean the same thing to all the people who share the same language and culture as you. But they may vary between different languages or cultures.

Other high-level involuntary gestures that we all use, such as touching our head to show regret — these are more likely to be evident when we have a good understanding of situations and a well-developed sense of empathy. None of this is possible without the basic communication skills that are the focus of this book.

4. Body position — think how much the attitude of your body communicates to others, for example lying down, getting up or standing on your toes.

5. Body posture — how you hold your body. Is your head bowed or raised, are you leaning towards or away from someone, are your arms folded or not?

6. Tension — this is very important in terms of recognising feeling or level of emotion. Think about the act of pointing at something or someone: even if we can't hear what is being said, the degree of tension in the body communicates different emotions — pointing with a stiff, straight arm and outstretched finger or clenched fist conveys something very different from a relaxed arm and open hand.

7. Gender — at a basic level, faces tells us the difference between men and women; they usually have different hairstyles; men have facial hair and, if they shave, their skin can be less smooth than women's. There are also subtle variations of shape and tone that tell us that a face is female or male.

In most instances we subconsciously combine a number of visual clues to make a judgement about the gender of an individual. Even at younger ages, it is important to know that girls generally look different from boys.

8. Proximity/personal boundaries — this is about learning how close to stand when talking to different people. We all establish our own personal boundaries, for different people and different situations. So our boundary with a stranger is likely to be wider than with a partner or friend.

We have to learn this through many situations where our parents or others have told us where and where not to stand, as well as through observation of others. Some parents and schools do not see it as a problem when a seven- or even ten-year-old still wishes to cling to adults. At a much earlier age than this your child needs to learn who she can stand very close to — ie it is not so appropriate at school with a teacher, but at home with you it is fine.

An even more complex level of understanding is required to know the situations where it is OK to hug a teacher and when it is not.

9. Body direction — this might seem too simplistic, but I have come across children who have not developed a sense of body direction. We must know that if a body is moving away from us, the back will usually be towards us and if the body is coming towards us we can see the face.

Standing too close
Look how the family are standing close to one another but keeping a distance from the man trying to sell them a car. In their subconscious, these children are noticing the difference and have a chance to learn for themselves where to stand.

This applies to such things as knowing which way a queue is going and is particularly important for group understanding — especially at school, where the children might not all be going in the same direction but the child needs to be alert to the general direction of most of them or the specific direction of his class.

10. Direction of hand and arm movements — specific movements are important as well, because they tell us a lot. Think of the following differences:

- putting a coat on a hook and taking it off
- lifting something up or putting it down
- taking a jumper off or putting it on
- doing up shoelaces or undoing them
- closing the lid of the saucepan or lifting it up to see if the potatoes are done.

These are just a few examples — we don't even have to think about them because the message is received and understood at a subconscious level. For instance, if you see your partner putting on their coat you know that they are nearly ready to go out with you and the conversation is likely to be about what you are going to be doing.

However, if you don't know the difference in the visual clues between putting on a coat or taking it off, you will not know how to make conversation that is relevant. Children who haven't learned this need to be taught it — I have had to teach 14-year-olds this skill!

11. Touch — how we touch each other and what touch means within a communication is another important aspect of body language for your child. Learning about touch is a huge area of development and in this book I will focus only on aspects relating to non-verbal understanding.

12. Relationships — it is most important that we recognise the relationship of the person we are speaking to — are they related to us or friends or strangers? How do they relate to others in the situation? There are physical clues from which we can make these judgements. This is how it is taught in the Not Just Talking intervention:

- Family members may look similar but are generally different ages.
- Friends look different but are about the same age.
- Strangers are people we have never seen or to whom we have not been introduced.

13. Clothes and equipment — these communicate a great deal because it is not only what clothes people are wearing but how they are wearing them that gives off non-verbal signals about context and relationships, even before you have spoken to them. Here are just a very few examples of how clothes can give us information:

- Whether a person is wearing smart or casual clothes, school uniform or swimwear tells us what they have been doing or are going to do.
- Whether clothes are wet or dry can tell us whether the person has been outside or not.
- Uniforms communicate what the person is going to be doing at work: nurses, doctors, dentists,

Direction of hand or arm movement
By looking at what this person is doing with her hands, we know she must doing up the laces. Undoing them would look very different.

pilots, shop assistants, postal workers, funeral workers, for example.

- Equipment also tells us what people do: plumber, electrician, gardener, car mechanic, etc.
- Wedding clothes and outfits for other formal occasions tell us what the situation is.
- Sports clothes communicate which sport you are going to take part in; horse-riding clothes are different from football kit or tennis clothes.

14. The way we wear clothes – this also gives us useful information:

- Smart clothes worn in a shabby manner can tell us about a person's frame of mind. For example if a girl arrived at school in a smart uniform but with her shirt and tie hanging out or her trousers looking like she has been to bed in them, would her teachers think that she is ready to work hard?
- Going to a wedding, people dress smartly, but on returning home after a day of celebration they will be more relaxed and may take off a jacket, loosen a tie or roll up their shirt sleeves.
- Sleeves that are pulled up or rolled down always communicate something – that the person is hot or cold, they are working hard or that they don't want to get their sleeves wet. The precise message depends on other (situational) clues.

15. Age – this is a very important part of interpretation and needs to be combined with other clues in order to make good sense of what we see. We need to know the age of the person to give them pertinent information – getting both the content and the style correct. A child who talks to her peers and her teachers in exactly the same manner will not be popular, particularly by the time she enters secondary school. Children need to know what tells them that someone is a grandparent or a parent or a teenager, etc.

I have found that virtually all the children on the Not Just Talking intervention programme were unable to tell the approximate age of the person they were looking at. This was because they had not learned to read clues such as hair

HOODWINKED

If a man wearing a policeman's outfit comes towards you in the dark, your reaction might be different from seeing someone in jeans with a hood obscuring their face. These clues are important but not definitive: without them you will be confused, but if you depend too much on them you may end up with the wrong conclusion – never judge a book by its cover! What these skills do give you over time is the ability to know when and when not to use them.

colour or complexion, nor did they understand the significance of this information in relation to age. When shown photos of people, they would either guess the age or count up the body with their fingers to see 'how tall' they were. They would say 'One, two, three, four ... they are ten', even when the picture was of an adult.

As will be evident from this long list, there are many signs your child needs to identify to make the best sense of what she sees. These are just the clues from body language! Did you think body language included all these aspects?

WHAT DO SITUATIONS TELL US?
Your child also has to learn the signs from the situation which, when combined with the information gained from bodies, will help her choose what to say and do. Only by learning the most common and basic interpretations can she learn to deal with the exceptions. Concentrate on giving her the basic skill, and she will do the rest.

The second key element of interpretation is to correctly understand the circumstances or the scene. Where is it? At home, work or school? Is it a hospital room or is it outdoors? If so, whereabouts?

Also at a higher level of interpretation, we need to understand what it is that tells us about the

This little boy has been watching his mum do her shopping. He is looking at the flowers, so when she talks about them he will hear the vocabulary and will associate it with the correct objects.

'MORE TEA, PHIL?'

In this simple phrase the message is supported by:

- an upward inflection in the voice – indicating a question
- eyebrows raised and/or head tilted in an interrogatory manner
- eye gaze directed at Phil
- finger pointing at the teacup
- teapot being lifted up
- cups and plates on the table, cups empty and so on – situational clues
- a pause – indicating a response is expected.

If you can't pick up some or all of these signals, you won't know it was a question or be able to give an appropriate response.

formality, informality, familiarity or intimacy of any situation we are in. A surprising number of children are incapable of making these sorts of judgements.

When assessing and working with older children, typically eight to 14 years of age, I have frequently been struck by how little experience and understanding they have of everyday activities or the language associated with them. This may be due to their behaviour being more challenging and their parents finding it easier to just get on and do things quickly. Many children simply miss out on this stage of development because they weren't 'joining in' earlier in their lives.

It is very important that babies and toddlers observe and participate in activities from the word go, so that they can accumulate knowledge about where exactly they are and then use it in other situations. Making sense of the situation shapes what we say, feel, think and do. So children who have not acquired this ability may be left with a profound sense of confusion and alienation.

You may be surprised to learn this. It is so easy to assume that children automatically understand the world in the same way as you do. As adults, we rarely need to talk about our understanding of situations. We don't say 'Look at all those dirty dishes — that means we must wash up'. We just make the assumption that everyone knows it is time to do the washing-up. More likely we will say 'You wash, I'll dry' or 'You load the dishwasher and I'll wash the pans'. We assume that the person we are talking to knows the following:

- we have just finished a meal
- washing-up is the next activity
- what the activity of washing-up involves
- the language associated with washing-up
- how to wash up
- the sequence of events
- what will happen at the end.

This understanding is only available to us if it has been stored in our subconscious since we were very young and built upon throughout our lives. This is why elders are revered in many cultures — their experience over many years helps them to evaluate and make the right judgement about complex situations. Because we use this subconscious understanding every day as part of all our conversations, we don't even have to think about it. We learn by observing, analysing, doing and comparing.

Your child accumulates this knowledge about what is happening in different circumstances between the toddler and pre-school stages. In doing so, she develops an understanding of everyday situations, which she can apply to new and unfamiliar settings. This 'database of information' develops in the following way:

- observing — watching others having conversations
- analysing — making sense of contextual clues
- doing — trying out what she has observed and interpreted

- comparing — assessing the response and learning what works.

Unless your child is able to do all these things based on what she is looking at, she will not develop the 'database' that will be useful throughout her life.

To be able to communicate effectively, the final element is that we must weigh the clues derived from both bodies and situations against our previous experience of similar events and locations. This is called the 'experiential' part of interpretation. Because we accumulate more and more experiences throughout our lives, these skills continue to improve as we get older.

YELLOW PAGES

Many advertising agencies understand the power of non-verbal communication. There is a wonderful *Yellow Pages* advert from around 2000 (find it easily on YouTube) starring James Nesbitt. It is a story about him being asked by his sister to get his niece's hair cut. He wants to save money, so he does it himself.

When his sister returns he pretends that a hairdresser has made a mess of the hair and then phones a hairdresser asking her to put it right. When he takes the daughter to the hairdresser, the sister waits outside in the car but can see what is going on through the shop window.

His body language looks as though he is remonstrating with the hairdresser but the words he is using give a completely different message about how he knows that she didn't make the mistake with the haircut but could she please help him out and put it right! His sister, therefore, continues to believe that the hairdresser messed up her daughter's hair.

CONVERSATIONAL SKILLS

Both speaker and listener play a part in ensuring that the conversation is maintained for as long as necessary. A conversation will die without each party possessing good skills in both these areas of development.

The essential conversational skills your child needs include the following:

1. understanding what a speaker and listener actually do to keep the conversation going

2. being able to reason and predict

3. prosodic skills — intonation, stress, rhythm, volume, speed.

There is more on all these skills in Part Three.

WHAT DOES A LISTENER NEED TO DO?

We all probably know that we need to look at the person we are listening to. But what does that actually mean, and how do we really know someone is listening? Here is a brief explanation:

1. The listener needs to look at the person — their face, not just their eyes, so they can see the whole body in their peripheral vision. This allows them to perceive the facial expressions and body language that will help them make best sense of what the speaker is saying.

2. The listener also needs to be relatively still. A person who fidgets or who moves about is hard to talk to and will find listening difficult.

3. Only if the listener makes a reply that is relevant to the topic will the speaker know that they are listening.

4. The listener also has to give feedback — either verbal or non-verbal — in order to let the speaker know whether or not they are interested in the topic, are following what is being said, need clarification, need more or different information etc.

5. This feedback from the listener includes asking for help if they become confused by what the speaker is saying (the message). The ability to seek help, to ask for clarification, is most important because in every conversation we are

TRY THIS YOURSELF

Firstly, look into someone's eyes while telling them something. Ask yourself these questions: 'How does it feel?', 'What else can I see?'

Now do the same thing but this time look at their face (focus on their nose if that is easier). Ask yourself the same questions. Looking at their face, you should be able to notice their whole body and it should also feel less 'threatening' for the listener.

also learning about how to understand the next conversation a bit better. If the listener lacks the ability or confidence to ask for help, then their skills will not grow in the required manner.

So a listener has be active, and this is done almost entirely at a subconscious level as most of it is conveyed through small changes in facial expression which, as we will see next, have to be picked up by the speaker.

WHAT DOES A SPEAKER NEED TO DO?
The speaker has to know that their message is understood by the listener. This is achieved by looking at the listener to see whether the listener:

- is interested in what is being said
- has understood, ie the vocabulary is right and the grammar is not too difficult
- needs more information
- has had sufficient information
- needs different information
- needs clarification
- is confused.

It is the speaker's job to adjust the message so it is clear enough for the listener and will be received with understanding. All the time we help each other out conversationally by adjusting what we say according to the non-verbal signals given by others. Children who are unable to signal that they need help miss out on this chance to make better sense of what is going on. Your child will need to practise picking up these signals a great deal to make sure his information meets the needs of his listener.

ADDITIONAL SKILLS
In addition to skills you might expect to be part of conversation, your child will have to develop skills less obviously associated with communication. Here I will talk about what they are, and later you will see their relevance to conversational skill development.

PREDICTION/ANTICIPATION
Being able to predict and anticipate what is going to happen are vital skills to prevent you becoming anxious or frustrated. This helps communication because when you are anxious, you do not feel confident, and we all communicate best when we feel confident.

Another benefit of learning to predict is that you will then have some idea what information your listener needs or will be interested in. If you can't predict, you won't be good at giving relevant information.

CHANGE
How a child deals with change will also have a big impact on his confidence. To recognise the signs of imminent change he needs to be able to identify and understand the start and finish signals. Children who can't deal with change opt out of new situations. There is also a strong link with prediction skills — develop these and the likelihood is that your child will be able to deal well with change.

Watching conversations
Sitting between his dad and his grandad, this boy can join in the conversation if he wants.

CHOOSING

The ability to make choices affects our confidence too, but it is also necessary because it offers your child a chance to communicate about what he wants and gives him practice at initiating information.

GENERALISATION

Once we are able to correctly use information from bodies and situations and reach conclusions by drawing on our previous experience, we start to generalise. This helps us relate what we have learned in one context and apply it effectively in another.

Children who are unable to do this have difficulty communicating and learning — it is a common symptom of children diagnosed as being on the autistic spectrum. However, when a child's interpretation skills improve he is likely to be able to generalise well in most areas of his life. This also applies to children considered to be autistic.

SPECULATION

From an early age this ability to 'speculate' as to what other people may be talking about, or what they are likely to do, will help your child learn how to use his past experience to good effect. Speculation helps him develop his skills to this high level. Once your child has a good level of non-verbal

Making a choice
This boy is trying to choose a book. If he hadn't developed the skill of 'choosing' as a toddler, he wouldn't be able to do this.

interpretational skill, he must develop the capacity to analyse information in any situation and relate it to his experience. Then he must speculate about two or three options of how he could respond in the situation and pick the most relevant.

Many children I have worked with are unable to speculate and, as a result, are unable to communicate effectively.

PROSODY

This covers the group of non-verbal signals that we use to modify and emphasise certain words in a phrase as we speak: intonation, rhythm, stress, volume and speed of talking, known as 'prosody'. Tuning into these variations and recognising their significance helps us develop a good understanding of meaning. Once we recognise these prosodic elements we can learn to use them. People who learn a foreign language but not the prosodic elements will speak the new language using the intonation and stress pattern of their mother tongue — hence you can easily identify

French or German speakers of English and vice versa for example, even if their use of language is good.

Our brains do not have the capacity to process spoken language at the rate at which we talk. In any sentence meaning is contained in certain key words and these are the ones your mind needs to focus on. The rest of the sentence is there to facilitate language. Prosody offers signposts to point your mind's attention to these key words.

Imagine trying to learn a new language from the radio, for instance Russian. If you were only able to listen to the radio and had no visual information to help you make sense of what you were hearing, I suspect you would get so frustrated in a short time that you might give up. You can understand the radio in your mother tongue because you recognise the stress pattern of that language and the intonation also helps you focus on the important words (information-carrying words — these are explained in Part Three, page 136).

But if you can't use the prosodic elements, as when first listening to a language that is unfamiliar to you, your attention is given equally to each word. In these circumstances your brain will become overloaded very quickly, and you will be confused and frustrated. These are the same feelings that children with poor non-verbal processing have most of the day, because they are only able to listen to the words and do not benefit from the 'prosodic' non-verbal elements of speech that would help them extract meaning.

WHAT ABOUT 'EYE CONTACT'?

The difference between looking at someone and making 'eye contact' is that the latter is something that is done to 'get to know someone better', to signal a particular level of interest in another person, and to reciprocate interest from them. Generally this skill is acquired in the teenage years so that you can get to know someone

of the opposite sex. It is a development made once many other conversational skills are in place.

In day-to-day conversations 'eye contact' is not generally necessary — people know how uncomfortable this level of interest can be under the wrong circumstances. However, we need to look at people when holding a conversation and as adults we generally look then look away at regular intervals.

But some children may not look at you at all or look away for too long while telling you something. Under these circumstances they may bombard you with information you don't require because they are not tuned into the feedback telling them you have had enough of that topic. This behaviour often indicates that children are only able to 'give' information and are not able to deal with supplementary questions.

For the purposes of this book the focus will be entirely on helping your child to be comfortable looking at the person he is talking or listening to.

AND FINALLY ...

The most important feature of conversational skill development is the interpretational skills. As we have seen, without these skills you will not know what to say and when, or even whether, to say it. Knowing how to interpret situations well will help your life prospects and make life experiences happier. But these skills are of little use unless you know how to be a good listener and speaker.

Happy days at school
Children at play school, focused and happy – just how you want your child to be.

PART TWO

A MODERN MALADY

Why is it that nowadays children are failing to develop skills in non-verbal communication — gesture, intonation, situational understanding, and so on? The simple answer is that, as we saw in the Introduction, the way we live our daily lives has changed and the things that once helped our babies develop these skills are no longer so readily available. Today's parents are given very little guidance on how to focus on activities that stimulate non-verbal communication skills.

HOW DO BABIES LEARN NON-VERBAL COMMUNICATION SKILLS?

Your baby will need to spend a great deal of time watching many different examples of people communicating face to face. She needs daily experience of observing competent communicators throughout the first five years of her life. In the past, nobody had to focus on developing non-verbal communication skills such as understanding and using body language and facial expression because they developed naturally alongside the progress of spoken communication. Even boys, who find this area of communication more of a challenge than girls, had time to develop these skills before entering school. Today, it is very different.

THE FIRST FEW HOURS

Many more babies now go into special care and can be separated from their parents for the first few days or weeks. By the time they are out of the incubator the babies may have lost the natural drive to look for faces, and parents will have to focus much more on encouraging this instinct. Most advice is to ensure bonding with your baby, but communication skills are more fundamental and should be your first concern. Bonding is only possible through communication.

THE WAY WE TALK TO OUR BABIES

In recent years 'baby talk' has had a bad press. However, as I will demonstrate, talking to your baby simply and with an exaggerated intonation pattern is the only way for her to learn to recognise

The benefit of facing your baby
The good news is that, in the past few years, parents are now buying prams and buggies that face the parent. See how the baby is almost at the same level as her mother. This means that she is easily able to see her mother talking to others, while having a good view of everything around her.

and understand many non-verbal methods of communicating. Only then will she be able to use non-verbal forms of communication.

Once your baby has learned to understand these big expressions, she can start to observe the subtle methods we use to express our emotions and you will then be able to use a more 'normal' style of talking.

FAMILY LIFE

As we saw in the Introduction, in the past non-verbal communication skills were mostly developed at the family meal table and in the pram. These were everyday opportunities for babies and toddlers to observe different types of conversations. Children who experience only

butcher, baker or chemist was an opportunity to talk to shopkeepers and friends — with the baby in the pram, at the right height, observing the different conversations.

TELEVISION — A NEW PERSPECTIVE
People's non-verbal communication is far too subtle for your baby to pick up on a TV screen and so, although she may appear to enjoy what she sees, TV will not help your baby make good sense of what is going on around her.

Try not to use TV to occupy your baby or very young toddlers. It is much better for her to watch and hear you talking about what you are doing. Your baby needs to see and learn from real people doing real things close to her.

AS YOUR CHILD GROWS
Playing every day with friends gives children the opportunity to broaden their experience of communication in its widest sense — which is useful for future situations. Nowadays, sadly, it is often thought to be unsafe for children to play outside for long periods unsupervised, but be aware that computers and TVs in their bedrooms take them away from the family, where they can learn so much from watching and participating in everyday situations. Try to maintain a variety of family activities and invite friends to play.

one type of conversation will grow up being able to communicate only in that one style. But to be effective, we must all be able to adapt our style to the people or circumstances that we encounter.

A baby does not come with a manual and, if you are on your own without your extended family nearby, it can be hard to know what's best to do. In the past, the extended family provided experience and support. Although children in single-parent families may have fewer opportunities to observe two-way conversations, with a little effort you can ensure they develop every bit as well as children brought up by two adults. You need have no concerns about using childminders: as long as they give your child sufficient opportunities to watch conversations, she will not be disadvantaged.

SHOPPING HABITS
Think about the way we shop. Now we shop in anonymous supermarkets where people rarely talk; we are pressed for time or we shop on the internet. This is a long way from the days when a visit to the

FOCUS POINTS

★ Changes in society have made it hard for babies to develop vital communication skills.

★ It doesn't really matter who babies watch as long as the conversations are close to them and they can see both sides.

★ TVs and computers do not help the development of essential communication skills.

THE FIRST 24 HOURS

A FASCINATION FOR FACES – HOW IT ALL BEGINS

Most of us know that babies are born with natural instincts. The palmar grasp reflex, for instance, when a baby curls his fingers around your finger in a tight grip, may be inherited from our tree-dwelling ancestors. But how many new parents know that in the first few hours after birth their baby also has an amazingly strong desire to look at faces? Or that this fascination for faces is a crucial first step in the development of skills that will enable him to communicate effectively for life?

THE MOMENT OF BIRTH

Immediately a baby is born he does two things, both of which are part and parcel of becoming a good communicator for the rest of his life. He starts to scream. By doing so he starts to breathe, but he is also learning to coordinate the movement of his vocal cords. If he is to be able to speak clearly later on, he will have to develop this control, along with the movement and coordination of his tongue, lips and soft palate, before he starts to use words.

When he has stopped screaming, the newborn baby starts to look around him. What he is looking for is anything face-shaped, that is, round, with lines and dots for features. He just wants to see faces, and it is important that you know how vital it is to encourage this interest.

When we see our baby search for faces, we cannot help but respond, but if for some reason your baby does not show any interest in faces, you must know what to do. But first let's understand why faces are so important.

WHY ARE FACES IMPORTANT?

Think what might happen if your five-year-old talked to his teacher in the way he talks to his

Look at me

This young baby is keen to look at faces while his grandad feeds him. During this feed alone he looked at his grandad's face for more than ten minutes. Do the sums for a baby who feeds up to eight or nine times a day!

eight-year-old sister. Think too about what might happen if he doesn't recognise when his teacher first begins to feel annoyed by his behaviour and only takes notice when she has got to the point of being absolutely furious. Life will not be easy for him.

Your child needs to be able to recognise the difference between a wide range of emotions, including happiness, sadness, boredom and anger. He also needs to understand degrees of emotion: are you a little bit sad or absolutely distraught? He must be able to tell the differences – and the similarities – in the way different people express the same feeling.

If he has learned to do all this by the time he meets his first teacher, he will recognise the signs of annoyance and will change his behaviour so that she is happy with him.

If your child is to learn these skills by the time he is about five, he needs to look at hundreds of different faces making hundreds of different expressions. He will need to see as many adults as possible make exaggeratedly happy, sad, bored and angry expressions – exaggerated because babies learn to recognise these feelings better if they are loud and obvious.

In other words, your baby needs to maintain the interest in faces that he has at birth. A baby's natural instinct to search for faces fades after 24 hours unless it is stimulated. So the more you can encourage your newborn child to look at faces in those first few hours after his birth the better. Of course, this may not always be practicable – perhaps because one or both of you is very sleepy after a difficult birth or because your baby is in an incubator. Don't worry – it is never too late to encourage your baby's interest in faces, but it is only during the first 24 hours that he will actually be looking for faces instinctively. After this the onus will be on you – his parents – to stimulate this interest. You should not give up until his interest is established.

Remember that you will need to make sure your baby is developing all the other non-verbal skills in this part of the book after being in special care for any length of time. If you can give attention to these now he will be more adept at learning the skills than when he is older.

HOW TO ENCOURAGE FACIAL INTEREST

Once things have settled down after the birth, hold your baby in front of you so that you are looking directly at his face. You need to be quite close to him, about 30cm (12in) away. When he looks at you, stick your tongue out at him. Repeat this expression a few times. As long as he is gazing intently at your face, he should gradually start to try to stick his tongue out, imitating your expressions. Your baby's vision is not developed enough at birth to make out fine detail but, even in the first day, he will be able to see the principal features of a face and he will observe this movement.

This exercise not only helps develop your baby's interest in faces, but also encourages imitation, which is another important communication skill. You can try sticking your tongue out at baby any time during the first two or three months, but in terms of encouraging facial interest and familiarity, the earlier you are able to do this the better.

Be sure to tell other people what you are doing and why your baby might stick his tongue out at them or you could cause a few other expressions from grandparents – raised eyebrows, for instance!

FOCUS POINTS

★ **There is a 24-hour window after birth when your baby is actively seeking out faces.**

★ **This instinct will fade if your baby is unable to do this for any reason, for example if he is too sleepy or in an incubator.**

★ **It is harder to reawaken this desire to look for faces, but once you realise how important it is, you can do it – so persevere.**

SIGN TO YOUR BABY

YOUR BABY LEARNS TO UNDERSTAND SIGNS

Signing — using signs made with your hands to represent words — can help you and your baby to communicate successfully in the time before she is able to understand and use words fluently. The first step is to teach your baby what the signs mean. You will find this is much easier than it sounds.

HOW DOES SIGNING HELP MY BABY UNDERSTAND WHAT I AM SAYING?

Until your baby is able to understand words, the only clues she has to what you are saying are your facial expressions, tone of voice and gestures. But these are sophisticated clues, and because she does not yet have the skill or experience to interpret them fully, she is not always able to make good sense of what is going on around her. Signing will help to bridge the gap until she is able to do so.

If, for example, your baby doesn't know that you are putting her in the car to drive home for tea, but thinks you are setting off to do some more shopping, she may well get upset or have a tantrum. Unable to use speech, she communicates her frustration and confusion in the only way she can — by crying and screaming. If, however, your baby understands that you are going to drive home for tea because she recognises the sign 'home', she is more likely to stay calm and contented (especially if that is what she wants to do!).

Babies can learn to understand signs such as 'home' and 'more' at a surprisingly young age.

TEACHING YOUR BABY

Start as early as possible (within the first month), making signs and saying the word associated with the sign. It is not necessary to use signs from

SOME SIGNS TO TRY

'MUMMY'

Middle three fingers of one hand tap palm of the other twice.

'DADDY'

With index and middle finger of one hand, tap the back of the index and middle finger of other hand twice.

'YES'

Closed hand nods up and down twice. Nod head at same time.

'NO'

Right closed hand twists emphatically to point forward as the head shakes.

programmes such as British Deaf Signs or Makaton. You can invent your own — your baby will stop using the signs as soon as she can talk. As long as you use the same sign each time you use a particular word, for example 'Daddy' when
Daddy is there or you are talking about Daddy, your baby will learn that this sign means Daddy.

Start with words that are meaningful to your baby. Make a list of words that she might need during a typical day. These must relate to real objects or people, for example 'Mummy', 'Daddy', 'bus', 'dinner', 'book'. There is no point in teaching your baby signs that she will hardly ever need to understand, like 'pencil' or 'ladder'. Words such as 'drink', 'food', 'nappy' and 'sleep' will also be useful for most babies.

The next stage is to introduce more advanced signs, like 'more', 'next', 'finished', 'time for'. These will help your baby learn how to predict what is going to happen next, a crucial communication skill.

'GOOD'

Closed hand with thumb up makes short forward movement.

'EAT'

Bunched hand makes two short movements to the mouth.

'SLEEP'

Head tilts slightly to rest on flat hand. Can also be both hands held palms together.

'NAPPY'

Fingers snap closed onto thumbs against sides of body.

WHAT IS YOUR BABY TRYING TO SAY?

THE FIRST ATTEMPT AT COMMUNICATION
Your baby will start to communicate from the earliest days of his life. He will do this through the sounds he makes, what he looks at and, as he begins to control the movements of his body, a range of gestures. Communication begins very subtly and grows each day as the interaction between you flourishes. Let him communicate — listen to him, watch him — and you will begin to understand what he is trying to say. Without words, he needs to use a variety of sounds to tell you what he means.

DISTINGUISH HIS DIFFERENT CRIES
Research has shown that babies are born with the ability to produce cries of differing pitch, volume, length and urgency. Each one means something different. Start to listen out for the differences. Does your baby cry in the same way when he's tired as he does when he's hungry or has a wet nappy? Listen to how he cries, preferably in a calm atmosphere, and you will begin to understand what he is telling you. You will soon know what he wants and will not have to try everything before you find out what he's really asking for! This will make your life, and your baby's, a lot calmer and easier.

LISTEN AND WAIT
Try not to rush to your baby whenever he starts to cry. Stop as you approach, and listen: is he quieter because he has heard you coming? Look around: is he cold because he has kicked off his blankets? Has something startled him? Is he wet and wanting a change of nappy? He needs your help to develop the ability to express different feelings. By not picking him up immediately you will be giving him that help: he will have the chance to develop his different cries and you will learn to recognise and respond to them.

Your baby also needs to practise crying in different ways to develop his vocal skills. He will need to exercise his vocal cords a lot as he grows. By the time he starts to talk, he will need to be able

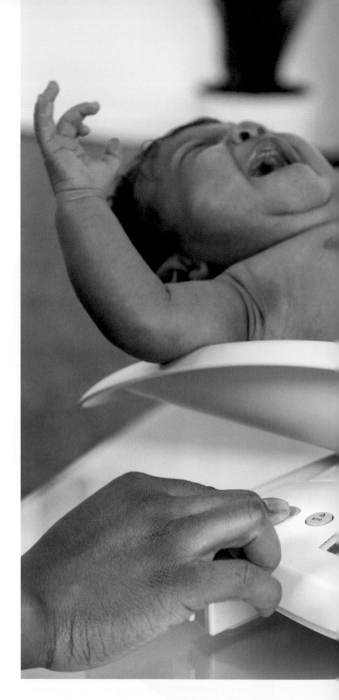

to control changes in the vibration of his vocal cords. This is also important because it helps him vary the tone and volume of his speech, a vital skill for effective communication.

NOTICE WHAT HE LOOKS AT
It is important to notice what your baby is looking at. When he looks around and tries to focus on

What is she trying to say to you?

This baby is crying. What is she trying to tell us? She is making a lot of fuss. Perhaps she's saying 'I don't like being weighed'? The sound of her screaming and her thrashing arms tell you something about how upset she is.

AS BABY STARTS TO MOVE ABOUT

Once your baby can move his body, his range of experiences will quickly expand. He will have different things to communicate about. Respond to these different situations in the following way:

● Each time you are able to make sense of the sound your baby is making — by noticing other, non-verbal clues, such as a damp nappy — use a word or short phrase to describe what is happening. For example you might say 'You're hurt' if he has hit himelf on something and is crying or, if he is being tickled, 'You're laughing'.

● Emphasise the main word in the phrase (in this case, 'hurt' or 'laughing') by saying it a bit louder than the other words. He will hear the emphasised word and link it to what is happening at the time you say it. Signing these words also helps reinforce what you are saying to him.

You need to be consistent in the words you use, so that he hears the same ones over and over again linked to the same or similar experiences. This will also apply when your baby is learning to talk.

something, talk about what he sees and what it does. Pick it up and show it to him. For example, if it's a toy car, say 'It's a yellow car' or 'It's like Mummy's car' or 'It goes beep beep'.

This will also give your baby the experience of initiating a conversation. He began by looking and you then responded by showing and talking. He is encouraged to do it again.

FOCUS POINTS

★ Stop and listen to your baby crying before picking him up.

★ Say what you think he is crying about — use the same words for each situation.

★ Watch what he is looking at and talk to him about it.

★ Keep the words simple in short sentences.

STRUCTURE AND ROUTINE

HELP BABY MAKE SENSE OF HER DAILY ROUTINE

Birth, for your baby, means entering a world of chaos. She will need to be able to make sense of what is happening around her if she is to communicate effectively. To do this, she will have to develop certain skills, such as recognising when things start and finish, and she will learn these more easily when there is a clear structure and routine in her life, leading to calm and predictability.

MAKING SENSE OF HER DAY

First, you need to help your baby understand what is going to be happening to her. You do not need to be rigid in your organisation, but providing some sort of structure and routine to the day will help your baby in many ways: it will help her to feel more secure, develop confidence and learn to predict, all of which are important for effective communication. Routine will help her to:

- recognise the common features of an activity such as feeding or nappy changing whenever or wherever it takes place
- understand the sequencing of events and make connections between them
- deal with changes and moving from one activity to another.

Structure is a clear way of showing the order of the day. So, for example, she learns that it is time to go to sleep when she is put in

Bath time
This is a perfect time to talk about what is happening and what will happen next. Draw her attention to the features of bath time, for example the taps, the water, soap and towel. Make up a bath time song!

her cot, kissed goodnight and the light goes off. Always put the same soft toy or teddy in the cot with her so that this toy becomes associated with bedtime and going to sleep. There is another benefit to this connection between 'teddy' and sleep, in that if you want your baby to sleep at her grandparents' or childminder's house then she will associate this new setting with sleep too.

Break your baby's day into sleeping, eating, nappy changing, bathing and other activities. The latter can be anything from going out for

Here it comes!
Hold the spoon in front of your baby's mouth, wait for her to open her mouth and say 'Here it comes!' Look at how this baby is focused on the spoon – she wants to eat.

a walk, lying on her back gazing at the ceiling or listening to a musical toy. One activity can be followed by another, fitted round her basic needs of sleeping, eating and nappy changing. Don't forget that she will want to play too!

WHAT IS SHE TRYING TO TELL YOU?

Your baby might be crying because she is hungry, wants her nappy changed or needs to sleep, but there may be other reasons. For example babies have a limited attention span and can easily be over-stimulated, which might make them cry. She might simply be trying to communicate that she wants to do something different. It doesn't necessarily mean she wants to move from the current activity to sleeping or eating; she might just want to do something more or less stimulating, or just plain different. When she shows signs of being restless or starts to cry, stop the activity and try something else. Maybe go for a walk or play a lap game with her. Or does she want to sleep? Just try different things.

START AND FINISH

Not knowing when something is beginning or ending makes your baby feel anxious. Being able to recognise the start and finish of activities helps her to stay calm. It is also one of the first steps towards prediction. When there is a clear structure to the day, there are plenty of opportunities to help your baby learn that things have a beginning and an end. Think of each activity your baby does as having a start and a finish.

Whenever you do something with your baby, for example changing her nappy, feeding her or taking her out for a walk, signal the beginning and end of the activity very clearly. The signal could be a sound, something your baby can see, or a word or phrase. As she grows, this will help her notice for herself the subtle clues that tell us that something has started and finished. Sometimes one activity can be broken into two or three elements – signal the start and finish of each of these different parts of the activity. Get into the habit of saying 'It's time for …', and at the end say '… is finished'. Also sign the name of the activity. See 'Sign to your baby' (pages 34–5) for more on signing.

STILL UNSETTLED?

If your baby is erratic in her habits, waking at night or feeding at irregular times, helping her to make better sense of the world through the structures recommended here should result in a better routine. If not, you might just need to be more consistent and keep the signals going a bit longer. Another option is cranial osteopathy.

CRANIAL OSTEOPATHY

If there has been a stressful birth and your baby is unsettled, is screaming or has colic, once you have checked with a doctor for other reasons for this, it is worth seeing a cranial osteopath. Cranial osteopathy is a very gentle treatment that can reduce stresses and strains and is especially useful with very young babies. The British Osteopathic Association will direct you to a registered osteopath.

TIME FOR MUM

It is really important for you to give yourself time on your own, even if only to sleep. So while your baby is asleep, you should make time for yourself and not feel compelled to clean the house. There might be a hundred things to do that can't be done while she is awake, but at one point in the day, at least, you need to make time to do something just to relax!

DEVELOPING AN INTEREST IN ROUTINE

Use phrases and rhymes to draw attention to the beginnings and ends of activities. When your baby is finishing her food, say 'All gone!' with an exaggerated tone, raising your arms above your head. When she is a bit older and you are clearing up toys, introduce this 'tidy-up' song, sung to the tune of 'Jingle Bells'.

Tidy up time!
These girls are having a great time with their toys. Soon they will need to tidy them away if they are to stay in their parents' 'good books'.

TIDY-UP SONG

Tidy-up, tidy-up, put the toys away
Tidy-up, tidy-up, we're finished for today
Oh, tidy-up, tidy-up, put the toys away
For we'll get them out again
The next time that we play.

FOCUS POINTS

★ Structure will help your baby make sense of a complex world.

★ Through structure, your baby learns to predict what is about to happen and will feel secure.

★ This will help her become an effective communicator later in life.

★ Signal in an obvious way the start and finish of anything your baby does.

★ Use rhymes and repeated phrases so she knows what is going to happen next.

GIVE AND TAKE

THE TWO-WAY PROCESS
OF CONVERSATIONS

Believe it or not, your baby will start learning how to hold conversations in the first few days and months of his life! He will do this through interaction – the two-way flow of looks, gestures, sounds and words between father and baby, sister and baby, and so on. This interaction begins when he has his first feed. During the first year of life he needs to enjoy interacting with others so that he develops the ability to communicate effectively.

THE ART OF CONVERSATION

Before your baby is able to talk he needs to learn about the give and take of conversations – how to wait his turn, how to respond to others and how to start a conversation. These skills are very subtle, but are the foundation of effective communication. They are difficult to acquire later in life, so the time you spend helping your baby now will be very well spent.

THE EARLY DAYS OF INTERACTING

As already seen, babies are very keen to look for faces. This is an important part of learning how to interact. He will watch and hear signals that tell him you are waiting for him to do something. Making faces and noises that interest your baby will encourage him to look at faces.

A good time to do this is when he is feeding. At the start of a feed your baby will suck without pausing but, once he has taken the edge off his hunger, he will pause now and then. The pauses will become more frequent and longer as the feed progresses. Your baby will look at you and you will look at him in return. Once he knows that his gaze will be returned, he will look for more opportunities to interact. He will start to enjoy sending a signal (the look he gives) and receiving a reply (when you look at him). Treasure these special times – you are helping to develop his conversational skills.

Always get close to your baby, so that he can see faces clearly: bend over his cot, get down on the floor with him, lift him on to your lap. When your baby is a bit older and is in a buggy or a bouncy chair, he may be low down or on the floor. Get down to his level or step back so that he can see your face and body better.

TAKING IT FURTHER

Once you are confident that he is interested in looking at you during a feed, start to make noises for him – perhaps cooing or humming sounds. Wait for him to reply. If he makes a noise in return, you should respond by making the same, or perhaps a different, noise.

It is important for your baby to know that what he 'says' is interesting to you. This imitation of the noises he makes is called 'mirroring' and will let your baby know that you value his attempts at communication – even if you do not always understand what he means.

These exchanges should be playful. Sometimes you will lead, sometimes you will follow the lead of your baby. This will encourage him to initiate communication as well as respond. You want him to be an independent communicator, so you need to stimulate both sides of the communication process. This will also encourage him to listen carefully – a vital skill for effective communication and learning.

FOCUS POINTS

★ Make contact with your baby during feeding – respond to him when he looks at you.

★ Enjoy interacting with your baby – make it fun!

★ Respond to his attempts to communicate by imitating the sounds he makes.

★ Practise these skills – they are the foundation for turn-taking in conversation.

ONE THING LEADS TO ANOTHER

We all know how anxious we feel when we can't predict what's going to happen, for example arriving in another country for the first time when you can't speak the language. Children who can't predict feel like this most of the time. And when we are anxious, communication is often the first thing to let us down: we become tongue-tied and struggle to express ourselves. To communicate successfully, your child must be able to predict what is going to happen next.

THE LEARNING CURVE

Your baby is not born with an ability to know what is going to happen next. She has to develop this very complex skill over the first few years of life.

Being able to predict will help your baby become a good communicator because:

- instead of feeling anxious about what might happen next, she will feel confident and therefore better able to communicate
- she will know how people might react to what she is about to say and will know what to say so that they don't get upset or cross.

TEACHING YOUR BABY TO PREDICT

The ability to predict will develop only if your baby has learned that one thing might lead to another. So what can we do to help our children know what is going to happen next?

Always talk about what you are going to do with your baby, keeping the language short and simple. For example, 'We're going to put your shoes on.' Repeat simple phrases at each stage of the activity, such as 'Here it comes, here it comes' when anticipating some food on a spoon.

It is very important to use a sing-song intonation, building up to the anticipated conclusion. You should also use this method when feeding solids, and at bath time and bedtime. You will recognise the signs that she can anticipate because she will stop crying, move her body in an excited way or shriek — all signs of expectation.

NURSERY RHYMES

Nursery rhymes are covered in more detail later (see pages 51–2), but here I want to emphasise their importance in the development of prediction.

Prediction is one of many skills that nursery rhymes teach because of the repetition of simple phrases. Your baby soon learns what happens in each one. Once she has reached this stage, you can leave out the ends of lines and your baby should fill them in, either by becoming excited or miming the associated action. Rhythm, intonation and stress are also important for signalling the end of the line.

TRY THIS!

This rhyme is particularly good for exaggerating information and if repeated often also helps with prediction.

Humpty Dumpty sat on a wall
Humpty Dumpty had a great fall
All the king's horses and all the king's men
Couldn't put Humpty together again!

FOCUS POINTS

★ Babies have to learn that one thing follows another.

★ Being able to predict reduces anxiety and helps us communicate well.

★ Talk to your baby about what is going to happen, using 'Here it comes' phrases.

★ Nursery rhymes help to develop a sense of expectation. Start with 'Round and round the garden'.

★ Babies learn to predict from stress intonation patterns used in games like 'Peek-a-boo'.

HOW TO ENHANCE PREDICTION SKILLS

Make fun out of situations that have different stages to them – nappy changing is ideal. It takes place several times every day and offers many opportunities to use 'Here it comes!' You should exaggerate your intonation as you speak to your baby through each stage. He will soon learn to predict what's about to happen.

Starting the activity
As you pick up your baby, tell him it's time to change his nappy. Throughout the process, it's very important to use a rhythmical intonation, stressing each stage and emphasising its final conclusion.

Taking off his trousers
Take his trousers off slowly. At each stage – undo the poppers, take his legs out – repeat 'Off come your trousers!' When they are fully off, say 'Trousers off!' and hold his legs up so your baby can see them without clothes on.

Cleaning his bottom
Begin by holding up the wipe so he can see it and then say 'Here comes the wipe!' Repeat this in two or three stages as the wipe gets closer and closer. Finally, say 'Now I'm cleaning your bottom!' and/or 'What a clean bottom!'

Putting on the new nappy
Be certain that your baby knows what is about to happen by letting him see the nappy moving towards him as you tell him 'Here it comes!'

Putting on his clothes
As you put his clothes back on, say 'On go the trousers!', 'Where are the socks?', 'Here are your socks!', 'Here they come, here they come, on your feet.'

MAKING SENSE OF IT ALL

DEVELOPING NON-VERBAL UNDERSTANDING

Once your baby is doing more than just sleeping and eating, he will become increasingly aware of what is happening around him. He needs to develop his non-verbal understanding through his everyday activities. Progress is relentless. You need a good idea of what to do next.

FACIAL EXPRESSIONS AGAIN!

We have already discussed your baby's first step towards learning what faces tell him. In his early years he needs not only to recognise the difference between facial expressions such as surprised and puzzled, but also to understand different levels of emotion, for example elated and content.

Your baby will have a much better chance of noticing these nuances if you exaggerate your expressions. Keeping expressions clear, even now that he is a bit older, will not hamper his communication development or be 'babying' him and, without this playful exaggeration, he might not notice the vital clues to help develop his skills.

There are some excellent board books that babies find fascinating by Margaret Miller and Roberta Grobel Intrater (see page 151). These will help your baby recognise facial expressions. Choose books with pictures of real people showing different emotions. Drawings or pictures of animals are not so good. If you can't get hold of books with photographs of people you could take your own pictures.

Nursery rhymes are also very helpful because most can be said or sung close to your baby's face, perhaps with him sitting on your lap. Another excellent feature is that they include exaggerated and sometimes unexpected facial expressions, as well as gestures and sounds to help your baby better understand what the face is saying. Nursery rhymes provide exactly the experience your baby needs. Don't be shy of singing them many times a day — the more the better.

Fascinating faces
Just look how engrossed this baby is in her book of pictures of babies making different faces.

MODELLING BEHAVIOUR

Your baby learns to understand and do things himself because he watches you so intently. What you are doing is 'modelling' behaviour to him. If he sees you do something, he is more likely to try it himself. Your baby will imitate any behaviour, including behaviour that will not help develop his communication skills, such as not looking at people when talking to them. So show him behaviour that you do want him to copy.

By now you will have made sure that he is looking at you most of the time. You need to encourage him to continue looking at people when they are talking to him. Whenever you speak to him, try to put your face at the same level as his. If he sees you doing this frequently enough he will learn that he must look at people when communicating.

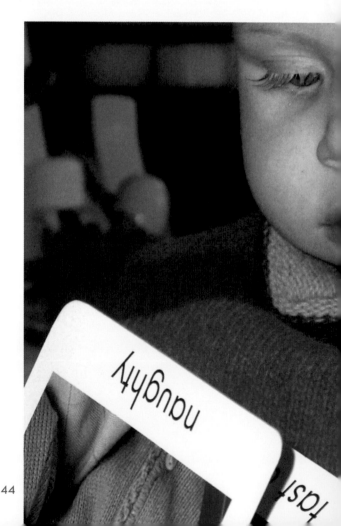

He will be building up his store of knowledge about the differences and similarities in facial expressions. It's important this is well developed by the time he starts school. If you talk to him and don't look at him, you are modelling behaviour that will restrict his ability to know what different types of facial expression and body language mean.

KEEP LANGUAGE SIMPLE AND CLEAR

Here are some tips to help your baby understand what you say to him:

- Keep the atmosphere calm and relatively quiet when you talk to him. If there is a lot of background sound, such as the TV or his siblings playing noisily, he won't be able to focus on what you are saying.
- Keep what you say short and simple: 'Daddy's

shoes' rather than 'Look over there, Daddy has left his shoes by the chair.' Again, this simple talk is not 'baby language'; it is the level of language he needs if he is to make sense of the barrage of speech sounds coming at him.

UNDERSTANDING SITUATIONS

Now your baby needs to recognise the clues that tell him what situation he is in, for example the bathroom or the garden. You should talk to him about what you see in these everyday locations. Draw his attention to the things that identify places and situations: 'Here we are in the bathroom. Look at the basin. Look at the bath. Here are the taps.' Point to each one and sign as you say the name.

When you see a different bathroom in someone else's house, talk about the similarities and the differences: 'Their bath is blue' or 'Look at the round basin.' He needs to understand the idea of 'bathroom' from common clues. He will then be able to recognise the same situation in different circumstances.

Don't forget how important structure is in helping your baby understand what is happening now and what will happen next. Clear visual signposts will help develop his understanding of the world.

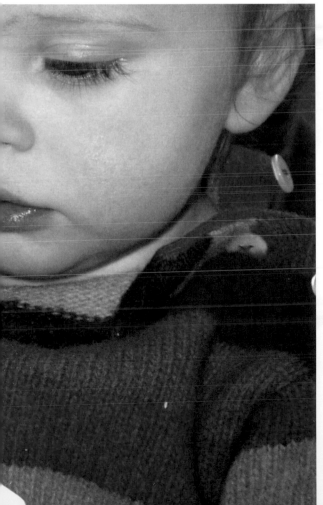

FOCUS POINTS

★ **Check that your baby looks at your face whenever you talk to him.**

★ **Show him photos of people making different expressions; talk about them and make the sounds that go with them, for example 'Yippee' or 'Hi!' or 'Yucky'.**

★ **Show him the gestures too.**

★ **Model the behaviour you want your baby to use.**

★ **Can he can recognise situations from the visual clues?**

BABY EQUIPMENT

HOW EQUIPMENT CAN HELP OR HINDER COMMUNICATION

Since the 1960s there have been enormous changes in the equipment used to transport babies and toddlers. These were made with the best intentions, to make life easier for parents or because it was thought that babies would develop interest in the world by facing forward in a pushchair. The fact is that, if babies are to develop the skills necessary to make sense of the world and to communicate with others, they need to spend as much time as possible watching adults in conversation.

CAN YOUR BABY SEE PEOPLE HOLDING CONVERSATIONS?

Whenever you are holding a conversation with someone, try to ensure your baby is present and can see both of you speaking and listening to one another. Before she is able to sit on her own, the only way of doing this is to carry her or hold her on your knee, but when she can sit by herself try to have her high enough to see you easily — a high chair is ideal or, when you are out and about, a pushchair with a seat that faces you.

THE BUGGY (AND ANY EQUIPMENT THAT KEEPS YOUR BABY AT KNEE HEIGHT)

Before the buggy (stroller) was invented, a baby — often until she was four or five years old — was likely to be in a pram, facing her parents. The introduction of the buggy made life easier for parents, but in a buggy the baby tends to face forward and, because she now had her back to her parents, she was not able to observe them engaged in everyday conversations. Of course, no one told parents about the impact on the development of non-verbal communication skills, so they were not able to make an informed choice; nor were they given advice on how to compensate for this key change.

It is probably the buggy more than anything else that has reduced the amount of time babies spend watching people hold conversations. Sitting in a pram, a baby can see her mother and, most likely, whoever she might be talking to. In a forward-facing buggy, the baby will at best see only one side of the conversation.

We have all seen parents pushing their baby in the buggy chatting away to their child while unable to see her face. Talking to a baby when you cannot see her face models to her that you don't need to look at people when holding conversations, moreover you will have no idea if she is listening to you. Babies learn most of their communication skills — both verbal and non-verbal — through watching people who are demonstrating good conversational skills.

Facing daddy
See how easy it is for this baby to look at his dad and vice versa. He is able to do this because his buggy faces the person pushing it and the seat is high up so the faces are closer together.

As we have seen, to become a good speaker and listener, your baby must learn that she has to look at the person she is talking to. If she doesn't, she will not be able to pick up the non-verbal clues in their conversation — a frown, a smile, a nod of the head, a wave of the hand. You need to show her how to do this by looking at her whenever you talk to her and letting her see your face when you talk to other people. Talking on your mobile phone might confuse your baby as she won't know who you are talking to — she could be forgiven for thinking you are talking to her!

To overcome the disadvantage of the forward-facing buggy, you need make only small changes in your behaviour. Whenever you hold a conversation with anyone while your baby is in the buggy, turn the buggy round so that your baby can see you both. Even when you are talking on the phone, make sure she can see you. If you are buying a buggy, keep in mind that a higher seat makes it easier for your baby to see your face and the faces of other people talking to you.

CAR SEATS

Another thing that limits the number of conversations your baby can watch is the fact that nowadays we depend heavily on our cars and don't walk as much as previous generations of parents. The car seat has been developed with the focus on safety. Rear-facing car seats in the front are a good choice for a new baby because she is able to look at your face while you are driving, but it won't be long before she has grown too big for a rear-facing seat. Also, these cannot be used in a car that has a passenger airbag — unless it can be switched off. (But do remember to turn it back on!)

Walking or taking the bus is not only better for the environment but gives more opportunities for conversation, which your baby can observe.

Lots of time to look at daddy
This father has chosen to sit in the back with his baby. A much better idea than the baby being in the back on his own. The baby can see his dad talking to the driver and to him.

FOCUS POINTS

★ Look at your baby when talking to her.

★ If necessary, turn the buggy so she can see people's faces.

★ Buggies that face the pusher are better than forward-facing strollers because your baby can watch while you talk to her and to other people.

★ Your baby needs to see all types of facial expressions – frowns, smiles and so on.

★ You should adjust your body position if your baby is low down, so that she can see you well.

KNOWING ME, KNOWING YOU

Your baby is not born knowing he is a unique being. He has to learn this in his first year of life. It happens gradually and he will demonstrate increased self-awareness by what he does, and eventually by what he says.

BECOMING SELF-AWARE

A baby's impulse to communicate begins with the understanding that he is a separate person. During the first few months of his life he will start to recognise the differences between the people close to him and then he will begin to see that he is a distinct person too. Unless this awareness that he is a separate person develops, he will not recognise that his thoughts are not shared by everyone else and that to be understood he has to communicate, to voice his thoughts. As he develops, the realisation that what he has in his mind is different from what is in the minds of other people will help him to know what he needs to say to them.

RECOGNISING HIMSELF AND OTHERS

Your baby is unlikely to recognise himself in a mirror during the first six months of life. He will see his reflection and might respond to it as an interesting person or image, but there is unlikely to be any sense of self-recognition.

You will also notice that at around six to twelve months your baby may cry and even scream at the prospect of being handed to an unfamiliar person. You may be worried that something is wrong or that he is going backwards in his skill development. Don't be. It is an important sign that he is developing new skills and awareness, indicating that he has started to recognise the real differences between people he knows well and strangers. In time he will cling to you less as he

That's me!

This baby pointed at herself in the mirror, then turned to her mother and pointed at the hairclip on her head. She then turned back to the mirror and pointed at herself. This demonstrated that she understood that the baby in the mirror was her.

develops his understanding of who he is and who his family and friends are.

INTRODUCE MIRRORS AND PHOTOS

Babies only learn by looking at things and making connections between what they see and what they think and feel. Your baby could go through his whole life without seeing himself if not for the presence of mirrors and photos. Both these things help him to start to recognise himself and develop a picture of himself as a person in his mind's eye. He begins to appreciate the distinction between himself and other people.

Very early on in your baby's life, start to play with mirrors — making sure you use safe, non-breakable mirrors sold by baby equipment shops. Sit in front of a mirror so you can see each other. Make faces at him, wave at him and draw attention to yourself by making loud noises such as 'coo-ee' or 'oo-hoo'. If you are out and about, whenever you pass a mirror or see your reflections in a window, you should wave at him and call his name. This will help him consolidate his memory of himself as a person.

The first person that your baby will learn to recognise in a mirror is you. You can notice whether or not he recognises himself (this usually starts to develop at around six to eight months) because he will smile when he sees you but may not pay any attention to his own image in the mirror. Only when your baby starts to look at himself, smiling and babbling — that is, trying to talk to himelf — or making faces at his reflection, will you know that he is on the way to recognising himself.

HOW TO EXTEND MIRROR PLAY

Talk to your baby about who he can see in the mirror — his brother, sister or aunt. Talk about what you see others doing in the mirror. Play peekaboo games, hiding your baby behind a cloth and pulling it off suddenly, or hiding your face from him with your hands, or hide behind something yourself and then suddenly appear in the mirror!

When your baby starts to try out different facial expressions or hand movements and looks at the mirror to check that the baby in the mirror is doing it as well, then there is no doubt that he knows it's himself he sees. Talk to your baby through the mirror: ask him what he wants for tea, or if he would like to change activity, maybe look at a book or build with bricks.

YOU AND ME

When talking to your baby, make special reference to anything to do with the idea of 'you' and 'me'. Draw attention to what you are doing or going to do and what you might be feeling or thinking, for example 'I am putting the forks in the dishwasher' or 'I think my teeth are dirty so I am brushing them'.

Talk about the same things in relation to your baby. Tell him what he is doing or what you think he might be feeling or thinking, for example 'You bumped your head. Is it hurting?' or 'Are you feeling thirsty? Do you want a drink?'

Talk about the same points in relationship to others in the family, for example 'Daddy is putting a jumper on — he must be cold. Are you cold, Daddy?' All of this will help him to see the differences in people and will continue to develop his ideas about himself and what he does.

MOVING AWAY FROM OTHERS

After he has learned to crawl or walk, your baby will start to move away from you in different situations. This is to test out how far he can go and still know that you will be there for him. This act of distancing himself from you is another demonstration that he is becoming aware that he is a separate entity. He will keep looking back at you to check you are still there.

MAKING PEOPLE LAUGH

Realising that he can make people laugh is another sign that your baby understands he is an individual. Repeating behaviour that gets a response he likes is an obvious sign that he is acquiring a sense of himself. Notice how he does something and laughs, then looks at you to see if you are laughing. He might make more of the joke or show it to someone

make others laugh, you should be pleased as it is a strong sign that he is starting to see the world from another's point of view.

SOMETHING MORE YOU CAN DO

You might like to make a photo album or scrapbook that is a record of your baby's life. With lots of photos of him full face and full body doing different things, he will soon learn to recognise himself. Also, compare photos of other people, tell him the names of the people in the photos, and talk about what they are doing. Use photos of people he is familiar with and repeat the same words each time, for example 'Daddy is swimming', 'Sarah is running'. Write these words under the pictures so that other people can use the same words.

It is difficult to find books with simple pictures of people doing things, but you could make your own. Perhaps you could make an album of Granny and Grandad working in the garden, doing the shopping, driving the car, eating lunch and so on.

To develop your baby's awareness of himself as an individual, talk about what others are doing and compare what you and your baby are doing.

I can make you laugh!
This baby is learning how to make people laugh. She is having fun with Peek-a-boo wherever she can!

else to see if that also produces a laugh. This is a clear indication that your baby knows others are thinking something different: he realises that perhaps you haven't laughed at the same time.

Help your baby develop this awareness by encouraging him to laugh about funny things that you do together. Once your baby knows he can

FOCUS POINTS

★ Your baby needs to learn who he is by first recognising his mum and dad.

★ Emphasise 'you' and 'me'.

★ Be happy when he becomes clingy, not wanting to be picked up by 'strangers' – it is a sign that this skill is developing well.

★ Use mirrors and photos to help your baby recognise the difference between himself and other people.

★ Watch him learn how to move away with confidence, knowing he can always come back.

ALL THE RIGHT INGREDIENTS

Nursery rhymes have all the components necessary for developing many non-verbal skills. Simply by singing or reciting nursery rhymes and playing lap games with your baby as often as you can you will be doing a huge amount to help her develop her communication skills.

WHAT MAKES NURSERY RHYMES SO IMPORTANT?

Nursery rhymes have been passed down from generation to generation and have always been popular. Babies and parents enjoy nursery rhymes and lap games — they are fun, help you bond with your baby and will also develop her confidence.

In the past, of course, TV filled less of our day than it does now (and there was only one programme a day for toddlers). Much of the time that parents and their young children spent together was taken up with nursery rhymes and lap games. Now research is proving how important these activities are, not only for the communication skills dealt with in this book but also in helping to develop pre-reading skills.

LOOK AT ME! WHAT AM I DOING?

Put your face close to your baby's face, sit her on your lap or in her high chair. From this position she can see not only what your face does but also what your body is doing. Start with just one or two nursery rhymes, for example 'Twinkle, twinkle, little star' or 'Incey Wincey Spider'. Find one that she really enjoys and repeat it often. She will not get bored. Do all the actions with her — some books of nursery rhymes show how to do these but you can always make up your own.

ENCOURAGING EXPECTATION AND PREDICTION

Because nursery rhymes are repetitive and engaging, your baby should soon recognise the different movements you make and what you are about to do. She will also learn to recognise a rising intonation pattern when reciting such rhymes as 'Round and round the garden' and will learn what to expect. This will also encourage her delight and you will know she is really learning how to anticipate.

Round and round the garden
Look how focused this baby is on her hand and her mummy's hand. After saying 'One step', pause and see whether your baby giggles in anticipation of the tickle under the arm. Say the words slowly and pause after 'two steps'. Encourage her delight.

DEVELOPING INTONATION PATTERNS, STRESS, VOLUME AND RHYTHM – PROSODY

Intonation patterns, stress and rhythm are the non-verbal clues that we add to words to reinforce the sense of what we are saying. They are the sound clues that make it possible for you to listen to the radio or talk on the telephone – situations when you cannot see the person talking.

Nursery rhymes help because all the intonation, stress and rhythm patterns are exaggerated, emphasised and repeated, so eventually your baby will learn them. Try 'This little piggy went to market', varying the intonation as much as you can and stressing 'market', 'home', and so on: 'This little piggy went to **market**, this little piggy stayed at **home**'.

Knowing when to talk loudly and when to be quiet is also understood through non-verbal signals, so do help your baby to understand the situations where you would be quiet or loud by making the non-verbal signals clear, for example 'Sssssshhhhh, Daddy's sleeping'. Whispering in your baby's ear from an early age is fun as well.

BECOMING A GOOD SPEAKER AND LISTENER

Nursery rhymes and lap games give your baby the chance to practise over and over again:

- looking at people
- sitting still to hear what is being said
- listening carefully
- asking for more.

These are all essential conversational skills and excellent reasons for doing nursery rhymes at least once a day.

TRY THIS!

Ten Fat Sausages

Recite this, do the actions and be amazed at how intently your child watches you.

'Ten fat sausages sizzling in a pan' (hold up ten fingers)

'One went …' (pop) (make a pop sound with a finger in your mouth – it is not possible to say 'pop' at the same time!)

'The other went…' (bang) (clap hands or bang on the table – again it is not necessary to say 'bang')

'Eight fat sausages sizzling in a pan' (hold up eight fingers)

Repeat the verse, beginning with 'Eight/Six/Four/Two fat sausages …', until …

'There were no fat sausages sizzling in a pan' (make a sad face and lift up your hands and say 'All gone!')

FOCUS POINTS

- Regular use of nursery rhymes and lap games with your baby can make a real difference to her ability to communicate effectively.

- If your baby doesn't seem to respond, don't give up. Just keep trying different rhymes until you find one that she really enjoys.

- Lap games, where there is movement and the opportunity to choose, are excellent.

- Exaggerate intonation patterns to make them interesting and noticeable.

- Does she enjoy nursery rhymes? She may prefer just one or two. If so, repeat them often.

EARLY USE OF NON-VERBAL SKILLS

EXPLORING TOUCH, GESTURE, VOICE AND FACIAL EXPRESSION

Alongside the development of other non-verbal skills, keep in mind that your baby will need to use his face and body to communicate to others effectively. This chapter will help you encourage your baby to respond to and use touch, facial expressions, vocalisations and gestures. All these simple things will also help your baby become a better listener as he grows up.

TOUCHY-FEELY

In this book touching means any touch that happens between two people. It often means touching hands or arms, but also sitting on laps. Nursery rhymes and lap games can play a huge role in your baby's learning how and when to touch.

Touching is a natural part of caring for your baby – for example while bathing him, changing his nappy and rubbing in creams to prevent nappy rash, or massaging him with oil. There is a lot of evidence that daily massage encourages interaction with your baby, helps relax your baby and reduces crying. The International Associate of Infant Massage (IAIM) offers courses for parents all over the UK http://www.iaim.org.uk and their recommended book is by Vimala McClure.

Through these everyday activities your baby will learn the meaning and pleasure of touch, and this will help him immensely later in life. Your baby needs to learn what touch means and how to touch others. This is a learning process that will continue right through to adolescence, when it becomes really important to know how to touch people in an acceptable way.

ENCOURAGE THE USE OF GESTURES

Gestures are general movements of the body that have meaning. To encourage your baby to use gestures you should make your body language large and noticeable. For example when saying 'Hello' and 'Goodbye', wave clearly; when your baby finishes his food, hold your hands up in the air

Sharing interest
This child has learned to point out things to others. Here he is pointing out the matching shape that he and his mum are looking at together.

above your head and say with a strong intonation pattern 'All gone!'; point to your body and say 'Me', then point to your baby and say 'You'. All these words and phrases should be said with a pleasing but exaggerated tone of voice.

HOW DOES YOUR BABY'S VOICE DEVELOP?

Your baby is born not knowing how to use his voice. During the period from birth until he learns to talk, he will have to exercise his vocal cords and all the muscles needed for speech if he is to start talking at some point between, approximately, 12 and 36 months. The crying, gurgling, laughing and cooing sounds that he makes from a very early age help him to gain fine control of his vocal cords.

If you don't rush to pick your baby up the moment he starts crying, you give him the chance to learn to vary his cry by using different pitch, intonation, volume and urgency. The ability to change these elements helps him express different meanings, and he will develop one cry for when he is hungry, one for when for he is in pain, one for when he is bored, and so on. Babies who are not given this opportunity early on to develop different cries may find it hard to vary their voice for speech later on.

When your baby coos and gurgles, you can help his voice develop first by copying any sounds he makes and then by encouraging him to try new or different ways of producing sounds — perhaps by changing the rhythm of your coo in response to him or by varying the length of the coo. As he becomes good at this, introduce different sounds. This is the precursor to babbling.

HELPING YOUR BABY BABBLE
Babbling refers to the noises that your baby starts to make from the age of about nine months. They are very different from the early gurgles and coos. They sound much more like speech, because the babble will show signs of the intonation pattern of your baby's mother tongue. Through babbling your baby will also learn to put consonants and vowels together and that, by repeating the syllables, the 'words' get longer — for example 'gah gah' and 'dee dah' (the latter also includes a change of sounds). This ability to combine syllables of different sounds is fundamental to the development of good articulation.

Babbling will help your baby develop the natural use of his lips, tongue and palate for articulation as well as his intonation, so that he will be adept at all these things by the time he is talking. There is more about babbling on page 61.

ENCOURAGE FACIAL EXPRESSIONS
Can your baby make facial expressions for himself? He needs to exercise his facial muscles to gain control and to make the necessary very fine movements. This can be done by making large, extravagant expressions to him; expand the range of expressions that he sees — thoughtful, worried, proud, excited and so on — and encourage him to imitate these. Exaggerate the expression to make it noticeable for your baby. And don't forget those nursery rhymes and lap games!

A GAME TO ENCOURAGE TOUCH AND GESTURE
I have played the lap game 'Hey, Little Fishy in the Sea' (see 'Try this!' above) with many children, and they have all loved it. Before your baby can talk, get him to point up, down or round when choosing.

TRY THIS!

… but not with children over four or five if you wish to preserve your back!

Hey, Little Fishy in the Sea
Pick the child up and get him to put his legs around your waist.

Tip his head down towards the floor and ask:

'Hey, little fishy in the sea, what do you want for your tea? Up, down or round?'

If he chooses 'up', throw him up in the air. For 'down', tumble him head over heels to the ground. For 'round', swirl him round like an aeroplane.

Finally, he gets the opportunity to ask 'more' — if you can stand it!

FOCUS POINTS

★ Touch your baby, and encourage him to feel your arms and face. Massage him as well.

★ Listen to your baby's cry from a very early stage. It will tell a lot about what your baby wants.

★ Exaggerate gestures such as waving goodbye and pointing.

★ Accept his babbling as attempts to communicate and encourage him to develop different sounds.

★ Can he imitate your facial expressions?

EATING TOGETHER

WHY FAMILY MEALTIMES ARE SO IMPORTANT

As your baby gets older, she will start to eat solids, and this will change the interaction while she feeds. She will soon be able to sit in a high chair at the table, rather than on your lap, which will significantly increase the number of opportunities she has to observe conversations taking place.

The process of eating is one of the richest areas of your baby's life for developing non-verbal conversational skills. This chapter will help you look at the family mealtime in a completely different way, showing how beneficial these everyday conversations are.

HOW CAN SPOON-FEEDING HELP CONVERSATION DEVELOP?

The transition to spoon-feeding should be another step towards your baby's enjoyment of food and eating. It will also bring plenty of opportunities for you to help her develop her interacting skills. As she finishes each spoonful, she will look at you and use gesture, vocalisation and facial expressions to let you know that she is enjoying

Eating round a table

This baby can see her father and brother eating their food. This is a good model for how she will need to sit and eat at the table when she is older. Also, she can see all the signs of starting and finishing a meal for three people – not just her own.

her food and wants some more. Alternatively, she might just spit it all out – which, of course, is her way of telling you that she does not want any more.

We have seen that prediction is an important skill, and one that you should promote in your baby. There is a great deal of prediction involved in the use of a spoon to feed your baby. Start by talking to your baby about filling the spoon – for example, say 'Look, yoghurt on the spoon.' As the spoon moves towards her mouth, say 'Here it comes … here it comes … and open wide.' Then add some words as the spoon goes into her mouth – perhaps something like 'Yum, yum.'

This is also a wonderful time to introduce the sign for 'more'. There are so many opportunities to ask her 'More?', and the sign is easily done by just touching the back of one hand each time you fill the spoon for her.

HOW DOES THE FAMILY MEAL TABLE HELP?

When your baby sits at the family meal table with lively conversation going on around her, she will see the smiles, frowns and looks of surprise that indicate people's feelings. She will notice how people lean forward to show interest in what someone is saying, use their hands to emphasise a point or lower their voice to share a secret – all the varieties of intonation and style that convey meaning and intention.

The way your baby learns is through watching adults and older brothers and sisters. This gives her an understanding of how to behave in different situations.

One of the most important things to model to your baby is that while communicating she must look at people. Think about this: when your family is sitting at the table and the older members are watching the TV, conversation takes second place. What you are demonstrating to your baby or a toddler in her high chair is that it is possible to eat, talk and watch the TV at the same time – without needing to look at the person you are talking to. So, please turn the TV off while eating at the table. Let the conversation flow!

SIGNAL THE BEGINNINGS AND ENDINGS OF ACTIVITIES

Making the beginning and end of activities very clear helps your baby learn to spot the less obvious clues that will, as she grows into a toddler, help her to predict what might happen next. In turn, this will make her confident and happy. She will see the start and finish of all her meals as long as she is sitting watching you while you are getting the meal ready. For more on this see page 122.

HELP YOUR BABY DEVELOP DIFFERENT CONVERSATIONAL STYLES

Because your baby is sitting watching a lot of conversations, she is going to see people communicating in a variety of ways: for example they may be happy, sad, enthusiastic, secretive or angry. From this she will learn that she needs to talk to people in different ways, depending on the person, the situation and what they are talking about. Babies who observe only one style of communication tend to communicate in a limited manner themselves.

FOCUS POINTS

★ Use 'Here it comes, here it comes' or 'Open wide, here comes a train' to signal the arrival of her food.

★ Help her understand the sign for 'more' by using it for virtually each spoonful.

★ Don't have a TV on in the room where you eat – babies can't learn non-verbal skills from the TV.

★ Make sure your baby watches the arrival and departure of different parts of the meal.

COPING WITH CHANGE

SOME COMPLEX SKILLS THAT YOUR BABY NEEDS TO MASTER

Your baby must learn that he is able to control his environment through communication and therefore doesn't need to resort to kicking and screaming. Imitation, choosing and understanding change are all skills that he will need to master if he is to understand what to do and say in different situations.

ENCOURAGE YOUR BABY TO IMITATE OTHERS

Imitating you simply means copying what you do. Babies can do this from the day they are born, but gradually they start to choose whether or not to copy. Babies need to copy facial expressions and hand and body movements as well as things like rhythms, intonation patterns and volume. This skill will also help your baby develop the ability to do new things. Respond positively to your baby's non-verbal communication so that he learns it has value and meaning and he will want to do it again.

NOW FOCUS ON CHOOSING

An important trait that develops around twelve months is the ability to point at objects and people. When he is a little bit older, this skill will help him ask for things before he can talk.

Once your baby can grab or point at things, he will be able to start choosing. Choosing is the ability to weigh up options and identify what you want to do. Humans become unhappy and frustrated when choice is taken away. Being able to choose will help your baby control his life and ensure that he is happy and content. Choosing is also valuable in that it gives him the opportunity to practise giving messages — a key conversational skill that will only develop with practice.

Your baby is not born knowing how to choose. He will need to be given opportunities to learn how to do so. Start early by offering choices of food and drink, toys and clothes. Then move on to choice of games or objects, things to do or places to go. Don't forget to sign while offering the choices (see right for a suggestion for a sign to use for 'choose').

WHY IS CHANGE SO IMPORTANT?

Within any conversation, people, situations and topics are likely to change many times. Your baby needs to learn how to deal with change very early in his life. Being able to do this may also prevent him having too many tantrums when he becomes a toddler.

Coping with change is not as easy as it sounds, and your child needs to be able to deal with both negative and positive change. Change can cause confusion, which in turn leads to stress and anxiety. This happens if you can't read the clues telling you that moving from one thing to another will be a good experience. Your child will also need to learn how to predict change: this develops from his ability to know when things start and finish.

TRY THIS!

A 'Choose' sign
Palm down, closed hand with little finger and thumb extended moves side to side.

A baby who finds it difficult to cope with change may cry a great deal, particularly when he is in new situations. A child who cannot predict change and deal effectively with it will become over-anxious during the change and may react in unexpected ways.

HOW TO TACKLE CHANGE

Make sure that change is signalled clearly. Start with positive changes. Your baby needs to be used to dealing with a happy change, such as having a treat instead of doing something else less interesting, or taking him to the swings when he thinks he is going to do something that he doesn't enjoy as much.

Early on use 'Oh dear!' (with exaggerated voice and facial expression) to indicate a negative change, for example 'Granny can't come' or 'Daddy is going to be late home.' Make a point of linking this to doing something else that is pleasurable: 'Granny can't come, so let's go to the park.'

LEADING ACTIONS AND GAMES

Your baby needs to learn that he can lead activities, for example in the bath or during play. Do this by encouraging him as often as possible to ask for things by pointing or, as soon as he is able, facial expressions. Always respond positively by giving him what he wants. This will encourage him to try to do it again — your baby needs lots of practice. He must develop ways of clearly saying 'yes' and 'no' — nodding and shaking his head, or using signs, for example.

Asking for toys

This baby has learned to sign and is able to make her own choices. Here she is telling her mummy 'I want to play with the toys.' She is happy and confident.

FOCUS POINTS

★ Help your baby copy facial expressions, gestures and so on. Have fun doing this.

★ Develop his ability to point so he will be able to choose.

★ Make sure changes are signalled clearly.

★ Be sure to give him opportunities to take the lead in nursery rhymes and games.

YOUR BABY STARTS SIGNING TOO

NOW SHE CAN TELL PEOPLE WHAT SHE WANTS

Very early in her life a baby learns how to communicate simple messages by crying, laughing, smiling and gurgling. But these are not precise methods of communicating, and your baby may show signs of frustration if you do not understand quickly enough exactly what it is that she wants. Teaching her how to make and use signs to tell you what she wants or needs will help to minimise her frustration and keep life calm.

SKILLS YOUR BABY MUST HAVE

There are certain things your baby must be able to do before she can begin learning to make signs. First, she must be able to understand signs. She must also be able to look at you for more than a few seconds at a time, so that she can learn how to copy the signs you make.

She must be able to copy actions you make with your hands or body: Can she wave back? Can she copy clapping? Nursery rhymes are an excellent way to find out how well your baby can copy you. And your baby must be able to manipulate her hands well. Can she, for example, isolate two fingers on one hand? Or make a pincer motion with her thumb and index finger? Is she able to point?

HOW WILL YOUR BABY LEARN TO MAKE THE SIGNS?

As soon as your baby is understanding signs, encourage her to make the signs herself — if she hasn't started already! Your baby wants to communicate with you and if you give her an effective way of doing so, she will. This is what you should do:

1. When your baby is screaming in her high chair and you know she understands signs such as 'drink' or 'nappy', say 'What do you want — drink or nappy?' At the same time, sign only the words 'drink' and 'nappy'. Keep things simple by giving her only two options at a time.

2. Encourage her to respond by signing and saying 'Drink, yes?' ('yes' and 'no' are key signs for your baby to learn).

3. Wait for her to copy you. If she indicates that a drink is what she wants, perhaps by pointing at the drink or getting excited, say: 'Poppy, sign "drink".'

WHAT CAN HAPPEN?

The Stuarts realised what a good thing signing was for their new baby boy and so started with a few signs when he first arrived — nappy, sleep, milk. Gradually during the next couple of months they realised that he had learned the meaning of these signs and as time went on they increased the number of signs they used with him — home, play, jigsaw, book, in fact anything that their baby did regularly.

Imagine their delight when at about nine months he started to try to make the signs and was soon telling them when he wanted his nappy changed and when he wanted to go home! He was a much happier child as a result and had fewer tantrums.

But the Williams family didn't find out about the benefits of signing from birth and so only started it when their baby was nine months old. He noticed the signs but took a lot longer to expand his vocabulary, so by the time his signs were adequate a few months later, he had started talking and didn't need to sign any more.

Because the Williams baby didn't learn the signs early enough he was not able to tell them what he wanted and, as a result, his parents experienced more frustration and temper tantrums in their child.

If she still doesn't sign, try taking her hand and making the sign with her. Then give her the drink. As long as she uses the same sign each time, don't worry if her sign is not exactly the same as the adult one.

If your baby is communicating well with signs, you must respond immediately. This teaches her that signing is the efficient way to communicate, and that it can be far more effective than crying. The next time you go through this process, she might well sign 'drink' straightaway. If you do not respond immediately, she will revert to screaming.

Once your baby starts to use signs, she might combine two, for example 'Daddy car'. This ability is very helpful when she starts to talk. She might also use signs combined with words to communicate longer phrases, which makes getting her message across much easier and is also excellent for her language development.

DOES SIGNING TEACH YOUR BABY OTHER SKILLS?
Signing helps babies develop one of the most vital skills in successful communication, the interpretation of facial expressions and body language. It will also improve her attention and listening skills because she learns the benefit of being still and focusing on communication.

Because you both have to look at each other when signing (or you miss the sign), signing will

Telling mum something
This baby is a good communicator although she cannot yet talk. She is telling her mother about something her mother can't see. She is signing 'Listen to the birds'. This demonstrates many conversational skills she has already acquired: initiating a message, self-awareness, good language at a two-word level.

naturally improve your baby's understanding of facial expression and body language. In order to recognise the signs you make, she has to focus her attention on your hands and body. At the same time, her peripheral vision will take in your face and the expressions you are making.

FOCUS POINTS

★ Help your baby copy hand movements.

★ Sign and say the words that go with what your baby is doing.

★ Respond to her signs immediately.

★ Your baby will learn to be a good speaker and listener if she signs before she talks.

GETTING READY TO TALK

HOW TO PREPARE FOR SPEAKING

So far this book has concentrated wholly on the non-verbal skills that are the foundation stones for the verbal language your child learns. Here we look specifically at how to help your baby practise making sounds — by focusing on his crying, cooing and babbling — and how to encourage him when those magical first words begin to flow.

THE CRYING

As we saw at the beginning of this section, your baby has to cry when he first starts to breathe — crying gets the vocal cords working. With that first effort comes the start of the ability to control the breath — delicate breath control is required for speech. And it is through crying that your baby will begin learning how to change the tone of his voice and expand the range of sounds he can use.

THE COOING AND BABBLING

We have already seen that cooing and babbling help develop his non-verbal methods of communication. Here you will see that they represent two further stages in your baby's learning to change the sound of his voice.

Cooing tends to involve vowel sounds only. Your baby will coo when he is feeling contented. He will look at you while he makes these gurgling sounds. It is important that you respond by imitating what he is doing. This will encourage him to do more cooing. Your aim should be to help him practise making sounds — not to teach him how to say words.

Babbling develops as your baby begins to play with sounds by putting them together, for example 'ma ma'. It is quite likely that your baby will use this 'm' sound first. In the early days of his life he spends most time on his back, looking up at the world, and in this position the easiest sound to make is 'm', because all he has to do is let his lips come together and let the sound come through them. He doesn't need to move his tongue at all.

However, once he can sit, his tongue will naturally fall behind the top teeth and, usually, the next sound you will hear is 'd'. Hence 'Mumma' and 'Dadda' are the names for the most important people in your baby's life!

Your baby now needs to develop fine control of his lips, tongue and soft palate, as well as his voice to be ready for talking when it begins. To help him, play lots of games babbling, doing things with lips, lowering and raising the tongue in the mouth and sticking it out to point it and move it sideways. Clicks and tuts are good exercise for the tongue, too. Don't forget to use the mirror to make this more fun!

Next your aim should be to encourage him to make all kinds of different sounds combined with vowels. You will be doing this by emphasising the vocal noises that we make during speech, for example 'daaaa', 'googoo', 'weee'. The ability to put these sounds together

Copy me!
Mum is saying and signing 'Look at the cat'. The girl is signing and looking at the cat '– soon she will be able to say the word 'cat' too. They are sharing information, an important skill for conversations.

in the right order is a very important skill that he will need to use as he starts to talk. Once he is putting different sounds together, your baby is well on the way to saying his first word.

PUT A NAME TO EVERYTHING

To encourage your baby to start using words to communicate, tell him, repeatedly, the names of objects or actions – you can do this from a very early age. Always use the same word for an object or action so he hears it over and over again, consistently. Eventually he will have a go at saying it himself. Gradually expand the type and range of words so he is understanding more and more words almost daily.

WHEN THE WORDS START COMING

There is a large variation in the age at which children start to talk. As long as the non-verbal skills are developing, there is no need to worry if your baby is not talking by the time he is two or even three. You certainly do not want him to start talking much earlier than one year. The shorter the time between birth and talking, the less time he will have to acquire the necessary non-verbal skills.

When he does start to say what sound like words, it is really important that you accept what he is saying even if it doesn't sound much like the target word. All you need to do is confirm what he is saying. For example, if he says 'da' for Daddy

Look what I can see!
This mum is pointing out what she can see underwater and the boy is looking too. He will see fish and be able to store what he sees in his memory associated with water and fun with his mum.

and uses it regularly for Daddy, then all you need to do is say 'Yes, Daddy', so that he can hear the word he is actually trying to say.

His listening skills are not fully developed yet and he probably thinks he is saying 'Daddy'. Gradually, as he listens more carefully to how adults say words, he will be able to make the same sounds. It is important that you say these words for him over and over again in a consistent fashion to help him remember what the word sounds like.

FOCUS POINTS

★ Encourage his babbling by copying him.

★ Develop his use of different sounds and combinations of sounds.

★ Always use the same words when you name objects and actions.

HOW TO TALK TO YOUR BABY

KEEP THINGS CLEAR AND SIMPLE
It is important not to talk to your baby as if she is an adult. 'Baby talk' — the language adults used to use with babies — had a vital role. It was instinctive, kept ideas simple and was at a level babies could pick up.

Exaggerate your tone of voice so your baby can learn to understand what different intonation patterns mean. Emphasise the important words, such as 'Car goes **brmmm**', 'Door goes **bang**', '**All** gone' (with a dropping intonation). Use a sing-song tone — 'la di dah di dah di dah' — even if the words are nonsense, like 'coochee coochee coo'.

Reciting nursery rhymes is an excellent way to expand your baby's understanding of different styles of communication.

SHOULD I TALK IN FULL SENTENCES?
At first, keep to as few words as possible: 'Mummy work', rather than 'Mummy's gone to work now.' Your baby will understand this more easily than a longer sentence. As it becomes clear that she is able to understand more, increase the number of words, for example 'Daddy's car, it goes brmmmm.' Because your baby watches many people talking, she will hear full sentences. By keeping sentences simple you help her.

Babies are not able to process a lot of words, so changing what you say will be confusing. Your language should be consistent, as well as simple.

DON'T ASK QUESTIONS WHEN THERE ISN'T A GENUINE CHOICE
Asking 'Do you want to go to bed?' when you are not really offering a choice is not a good idea as it invites the answer 'Yes' or 'No' — and you may get the answer you don't want! It is much better to tell her what is going to happen: 'It's time for bed.' Then the last word she hears always goes with the activity.

THE USE OF 'PLEASE' AND 'THANK YOU'
Insisting on your child saying 'please' and 'thank you' can block her understanding. Children do not learn what these words mean until they are about four or five. Before that, she'll repeat them, learned by rote, because you want her to and without knowing what the words mean. Also, if she is slow to talk, she may find saying 'please' is a way of getting everything she wants without needing to learn many other words.

COMBINING WORDS AND SIGNS
When you sign to your baby, always say the words associated with the sign. That way, she will connect the sound of the word, the sign and the object, and will learn to produce the word herself more quickly.

REACT TO ACTIONS AND EVENTS
Some words seem to have gone out of common use with babies — like 'Uh oh!', 'Oops a daisy', 'Yucky', 'Yum yum'. But they are very helpful for learning to understand how people are feeling.

TRY THIS!

Feeling worried is an emotion your baby will see and needs to know later. To help her learn what a worried expression looks like, show her the picture of a baby looking worried in Margaret Miller's *Baby Faces*. Say 'Uh oh! Trouble!' and talk about why the baby might be worried. Then, when there's an accident — maybe water splashing out of the bath — say 'Uh oh! Trouble'. Your baby will enjoy this. Don't forget to talk about what caused the 'trouble'.

FOCUS POINTS

★ **Make your message clear.**

★ **Model how a word should sound. Don't correct your baby.**

★ **Encourage your baby to put words and signs together.**

PART THREE

FROM TALKING TO SCHOOL ENTRY

As we have already seen, it is important to give your child support to encourage his non-verbal communication skills. This section will help you understand more about the way these develop after he starts talking so that you can take steps to promote them in your child. Good communication skills will help your child understand and deal with events and situations in his daily life.

The progress your child makes once he starts talking underpins all his conversations. Without these skills, he will find communicating problematic. He will be able to talk but not understand what others want to hear or expect him to do.

A GREAT LEAP FORWARD

Your child started to develop good communication skills as a baby because, among other things, you used signing and clear, simple spoken language to be sure he picked up the non-verbal clues and non-verbal language. Now, as a toddler, he is on the verge of using spoken language to help him communicate effectively for the rest of his life.

Before school entry, your child will need to develop sufficient conversational skills to ensure that he will make full use of the language he is learning. If he doesn't, he may be at risk of not knowing what people are saying to him or how to behave at school. Language develops automatically with every conversation that he holds, so make it your goal to help him to hold conversations in increasingly demanding situations and you will also help his language develop well.

However, if you encourage his language skills at the expense of the non-verbal conversational skills that are recommended in this section, you may find that, although he develops excellent spoken language, his non-verbal ability is

inadequate. As a result, from as early as three, he will be at risk of experiencing the following:

- failure to communicate effectively in all situations
- inappropriate behaviour, which may be exacerbated on school entry
- underachievement at school
- an inability to make and keep friends
- poor understanding of other people's emotions
- inability to communicate his own emotions effectively
- lack of confidence in his communication
- inability to predict well, resulting in anxiety and confusion, often from moment to moment, resulting in poor self-esteem.

This lack of skills may not have a big impact at primary school, although there could be circumstances in which he finds certain situations

Joining in

Look at this baby looking at her cousin. Even at such an early stage, she is fascinated with faces! This was her 'naming day' and many other people attended – all of whom she watched with interest.

difficult. These problems often occur more at home than in school. That is, he might behave well at school but be a nightmare at home. Most of the children I see are referred to me by their parents because of problems at home, but it is also possible for school to be the more challenging situation for the child; entry to secondary school is without doubt the time your child will find most difficult.

At secondary level, non-verbal skills become vital and children who do not understand what is happening or expected of them because they do not pick up the clues may quickly find themselves at odds with school life. They may be excluded or, because of their anxiety, may refuse to attend.

If your child functions well in some situations but not others, he cannot be on the autistic spectrum. Autism is a 'pervasive' disorder — which in lay terms means it is there all the time. You cannot be autistic at home but not at school, even though some professionals appear to suggest you can.

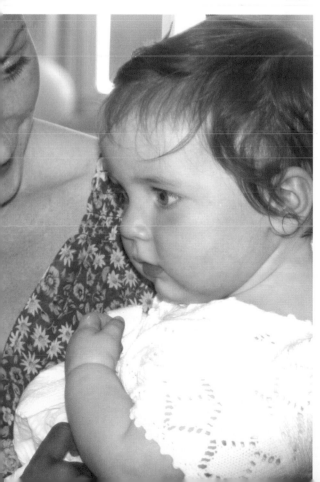

The explanation is that his interpretational skills are not good enough to cope in all situations — so they may work well at school because of the structure of the daily routine, but not at home, where things are less predictable. This variation in his behaviour may confuse the child, the parents and the professionals.

THE ESSENTIAL CONVERSATIONAL SKILLS
Now that your child is older, you need to focus on the more advanced skills he needs in order to hold good conversations. These include:

● How he understands the more complex clues given by faces, bodies and situations, including the different levels at which each emotion can be communicated.
● What a speaker does to start and maintain a conversation:

  ○ how he makes sure the level and amount of information are suitable for his listener
  ○ how he tells whether what he says is of interest to the listener.

● What the listener does in a conversation to keep it going.
● How the listener role changes to the speaker role, and vice versa, at different times during the conversation.
● Other related skills, such as prediction, drawing conclusions, making choices and seeing hidden meanings.
● The language skills he will need to accompany his non-verbal conversational skills.

All these elements develop alongside each other, so one chapter doesn't necessarily flow into another chronologically. However, I have covered the most important conversational skills first in the knowledge that language develops naturally alongside these vital skills.

If your child enters school with any of these non-verbal skills missing, he will find making adequate progress — both academically and socially — very challenging. However, you can prevent this by following the advice in this part of the book.

NOW LOOK WHO'S TALKING!

It is perfectly natural for parents to be eager to hear their child talk and see what he sounds like, particularly when it's their first child. It is an understandable assumption that their child's first word signals that talking and, therefore, communication are about to take off. However, the way we live our lives has changed significantly over recent decades and it is now recognised that learning to communicate starts well before speech.

HER FIRST WORDS

Usually words start to appear between the ages of 12 and 36 months, but it could be earlier or later than this. Your child needs a long period — at least 12 months — in which to develop and use her non-verbal understanding before she starts to talk. If the period is too short, her non-verbal communication may not keep pace with her spoken language.

The problems associated with talking later (24–36 months) are mainly to do with the accuracy of articulation, because your child hasn't been attempting to pronounce words daily for the past two or three years. However, her non-verbal communication skills need to develop well during the time before she starts speaking. You can confirm this by assessing whether she can:

- understand what is said to her
- recognise what is happening from the visual clues
- predict what will happen next in different situations
- use a range of facial expressions and body language in a meaningful way
- get her message across without the need for spoken language in most situations.

If she can do all these things, then you should have no real concern. However, if she still doesn't talk, you should seek a referral for her to speech and language therapy. This should help rule out significant problems associated with verbal understanding and any more serious problems with spoken language or speech sound production that might account for the failure to develop speech.

Children with normally developing non-verbal communication skills will start to talk when these skills are sufficient to underpin the verbal message. Once your child has uttered her first word or words, encourage her to produce new words by pointing to objects, actions and people and saying what it is, clearly emphasising the name (noun).For example 'There's a car' or 'That's a hat' or 'Food'. In time, these few first words will turn into two- and three-word phrases and then sentences.

As your child begins to say her first words, help her to expand on the non-verbal skills she has developed so far. Once speaking takes over, it is easy to assume that all is well and you could find yourself focusing on her spoken language without realising that she may be missing non-verbal processing skills.

In the days when children were constantly exposed to everyday opportunities to learn non-verbal skills — family mealtimes and going out to play with their peers and so on (see Sue Palmer's book *Toxic Childhood*) — development occurred naturally. Now, you need to check that your child understands all she needs to.

SIGNING TO TALKING

If you have signed to your baby from birth, she may well be signing two or three words together by the time she starts to talk. She will already have knowledge of the language skills that will come into play, so she may understand the difference between the name of an object, such as 'dog', and an activity, such as 'play'.

As words start to appear, the length of these 'sentences' that she has produced by combining signs could suddenly increase because she adds in the one word that she is now able to say; for instance she says 'Daddy' and then signs 'car' and 'home'. So from one spoken word she is able to communicate in a three-word sentence!

Gradually, as more spoken words appear, your child will drop the signing until she is using only speech, with more and more words put

Chatting to an adult
This little girl is in a nursery chatting to an assistant at playgroup about the shapes they are playing with. Look at how focused she is on looking at the assistant.

together. Talking is a much more effective method of communication than signing. This will happen naturally and doesn't need encouraging. If she keeps on using the signs for longer than you expect, it is because her non-verbal skills are not keeping pace with her spoken language. Don't worry about the signing taking a long time to disappear. As soon as talking becomes more useful to her she will have no need to sign because it is much more effort than speaking!

CAN YOU UNDERSTAND HER?
Even if you can't understand the words that your child uses at this early stage of talking, don't worry or make a big fuss about how she pronounces the words. As long as you can make sense of what she is saying you should not need to seek outside help. You are familiar with her unusual way of saying words because she uses the same word over and

over again for an object or action. For example she says 'jajas' for pyjamas. As long as she is joining in conversations and is really listening to how these words are said, she will soon start to change her 'idiosyncratic' way of saying 'jajas' into the adult form of the word.

However, if each time she says her word for 'pyjamas' it is different and you can't easily understand it, then you are likely to need the help of a speech and language therapist.

FOCUS POINTS

★ Encourage signing.

★ Accept how she says words. Just repeat them clearly for her to notice the difference between what you say and her pronunciation.

★ Encourage her to put words together to make short sentences.

WHAT DOES THAT MEAN?

This chapter is about the great importance of making the same sense of visual clues as everyone else. Without this skill you would not be able to talk in a way that is both relevant to the people you are with and compatible with the situation you are in. You will see how much information even a simple set of circumstances contains and how complicated interpretation can be. Interpreting visual clues in the same way as other people helps you decide:

- what to say
- whether to say it
- when to say something
- how to say it — ie, which vocabulary to use and in what style — formal or informal, etc
- how to behave
- what to feel
- what others feel.

So the continued development of your child's interpretational skills is vital to ensure that he will be a competent communicator. In this chapter I will show you how he should develop his understanding and use of facial expressions, body language and other related areas of interpretation.

GET READY, GET SET
Can your child do all the following by the time he enters school?

- Read the information contained in facial expressions and body language.
- Identify from the significant clues what is going to happen in the situation — ignoring unhelpful or irrelevant clues.
- Relate what he sees to his past experience of similar situations.

He should also use each of these sources of information — body language, contextual clues

Boys versus girl faces
You might think these four children are boys if you simply look at their clothes. However, noticing that two have hair cuts round their ears and the other two have more girl-like haircuts and 'prettier' faces, will help you decide that two are boys and two are girls.

and past experience – in equal measure. If one element dominates another, he will not make good sense of what he needs to do and say, and he may not talk about the same thing as other people in the same situation. When he is able to process all three pieces of information adequately, he must think of two or three options for communication or behaviour, for example 'Is it best to fish the ball out of the river with a stick or wade into the river to get the ball or shall I ask a grown up to get it for me?' Based on what he sees and his past experiences, your child should be able to pick the appropriate behaviour for the situation. If he only has one choice of what to do, then it might not be the right choice!

Only when he is competent at using all three of these elements, will he understand what is happening in most of the situations he encounters and be able to respond to each one quickly and accurately. Sometimes it might be just too complicated and difficult for him to make any sense – this happens in adult life too – but, because you have made sure all his conversational skills are well developed, he will be able to ask others for help.

BODY LANGUAGE AND FACIAL EXPRESSIONS
On the following pages you will learn about the complexity of the information that in an instant tells us who it is we are talking to and, therefore, the information that they are likely to need. This is not about making judgements on people; it is simply about gathering some basic details – for example what people are wearing, their appearance, attitude and posture – in order to adjust the topic and the style of communication appropriately.

READING FACES AND HEADS
Our faces convey a wealth of information. Think of the expressions that overtly communicate emotions such as 'happiness', 'confusion', 'worry'. Think too of the more nuanced expressions for 'attentiveness' or 'uninterest'. I will cover complex non-verbal messages such as sarcasm and innuendo later in the book.

Whenever you, as an adult, look at someone's face you are subconsciously calculating the age, gender, health and emotional state of that person. This directly influences the way you respond. Your child needs to develop this skill, at a simple level, from an early age. Here are some ideas for you to try with him:

1. Check that your child can tell the difference, by looking at their faces, between not only men and women but also boys and girls. The former is easier because you can help your child to see that men either have evidence that they shave or have moustaches or beards. Also, men's skin tends not to be as smooth as women's – generally!

2. It is sometimes slightly harder to identify whether a child is male or female, so make a point of talking about the difference between boys' hair, which (for these purposes) is cut round the ears and short at the back, and girls' hair, which is generally left to grow longer.

3. There are differences between boys' and girls' faces, but these can be variable and harder to detect. This is another reason why your child needs to look at many faces from an early age. He must identify the indistinct clues that indicate that a girl's face tends to be slightly 'prettier' than a boy's. There is something 'girly' about girls and something 'boyish' about boys! This is hard to put into words, but it may be something to do with girls having longer eyelashes, fuller lips, more delicate noses or perhaps slightly more oval faces.

Adults know all this subconsciously and are able to spot the difference without even thinking about it. With your help, your child will learn to do this too. Of course, we use other details, such as the person's clothes, what they are doing or the topic of conversation, to back up the hunch we get when we first look at the person. Usually, however, we begin to draw a conclusion from the face and then the other clues just help to confirm or contradict it.

As with all these non-verbal communication skills, it is important that you talk to your child about what's going through your mind so that he can hear what you think and make a connection to what is happening. Talk about why someone looks like a man or a woman, a boy or a girl. Point out the clues that tell you this, saying something like 'I see her long hair and her pretty face and this makes me think she is a girl.' Then your child has a chance to use this information for himself when you are not there to help him.

This approach may sound simplistic, but unless your child understands the most common or general features of gender recognition, he won't be able to acquire an understanding of variations and exceptions later on.

HOW OLD ARE YOU?

It is important to be able to identify the age of the person we are talking to because this helps us know what to say. We do this mostly by looking at the head and face, but we also pick up other clues from other parts of the body.

Help your child recognise the change in appearance as people grow older. Your child won't learn all these signals at once, but by talking to him about these ways of looking at people, you will help him become more observant and start to make connections.

1. Newborn babies can't do anything for themselves – they have virtually no control of their limbs.

2. Slightly older babies have learned to sit and use their arms for reaching and grasping.

3. Older babies whose legs and feet are turned out don't look able to walk yet, and those whose

Old people clues
The almost white hair and deeper wrinkles tell us that these two are grandparent age and probably in their seventies.

feet are facing forward look as though they have the potential to walk soon.

4. Toddlers — who look like they have only just learned to walk or run — are slower, tend to waddle and may look unsteady.

5. On the other hand, five- or six-year-olds tend to be good at running, walking and jumping!

6. Toddlers tend to look a bit more 'chubby' of face, arms and legs compared with a six-year-old. You can even see this in their fingers.

7. Reception or first-year primary children can be compared with children of seven to nine years. This is hard for your child, as the difference in age is mostly to do with older children having more mature-looking faces, but if you compare lots of children, he will start to recognise the difference for himself.

8. To pick up the age of teenagers, think about the difference in boys between early and mid-teens because of the appearance of hair on their faces, and talk about girls who go from being completely flat chested to developing breasts.

9. In their mid-teens boys and girls also tend to start wearing clothes that are likely to be attractive to the opposite sex.

10. In the late teens boys will show evidence of starting to shave, while girls may start wearing make-up.

11. People in their twenties have very smooth faces (except for men), arms and legs. Their faces still look young. If you try comparing some 20- and 30-year-old faces for yourself, you will be better able to help point out these differences to your child.

12. Men in their twenties tend to show signs of shaving — point out to your child the shadow or bristles on his dad's face. Let him feel the difference between his dad's face before and after shaving.

13. Women in their mid- to late teens and early twenties start to wear jewellery, manicure and paint their nails, and wear make-up.

14. People in their thirties usually still have fairly wrinkle-free skin, but their faces generally look more mature than people in their twenties. Again, only by looking at a lot of faces will your child get a feel for this.

15. More noticeable changes start to take place in our forties: there are signs of some wrinkles appearing, the veins on the backs of hands become more prominent, and there can also be some evidence of hair beginning to go grey.

16. These signs become more obvious in the fifties, particularly the tendency to have more grey hair.

17. The wrinkles are well established in the sixties and most people will now have grey hair. Point out that some women try to hide this by dyeing their hair, but it is still possible to identify their age because skin loses its elasticity. The skin on the backs of the hands, in particular, wrinkles and the veins become much more prominent. Show

him how elastic his own skin is and how slowly the skin of a 50-year-old or older person takes to return to being flat after being stretched!

18. Another sign of age is that our ears (and noses), keep on growing for ever and as a result will be larger throughout the next two or three decades. By the time people are in their eighties their ears can be quite large!

19. Hair tends to become almost white between the age of 70 and 80. You can also help your child look for more and deeper wrinkles. There will also be clues in the hands, which may be less flexible or bent with arthritis.

20. An elderly person may be fit or frail. Again, this is a complex judgement based on our non-verbal understanding of what a frail grandparent or neighbour looks like. But in my experience children start to notice this if you draw their attention to it in the manner suggested in the box below.

21. Finally, check your child understands that height doesn't always indicate age: give him

HOW TO HELP YOUR CHILD

Make comments and ask questions about people's ages, for example:

- 'Does that boy look like he could run or has he just learned to walk?'
- 'Is that girl's face still chubby?'
- 'Has that boy started to shave yet?'
- 'Is that person a Daddy or a Grandpa?'
- 'Is that Granny fit or frail?' – if he doesn't know, try asking 'Do you think she is able to ride a bike or mow the lawn?' or 'Does she look like she might have trouble walking?'
- 'Has that person got a few wrinkles or lots of wrinkles?'
- 'How deep are that person's wrinkles?'
- 'Is that person's hair a little bit grey or nearly white?'

The way to be certain that your child is good at knowing people's ages is to say:

1. 'How old do you think that person is?' – indicating the person you refer to (do this with people you know first!).

2. If he can't tell you, you might say:
- 'Is she three or ten?' Make the difference between the two ages large so he is more likely to pick the right one. As he gets better at this, make the difference less, for example three or six.
- 'I see their grey hair and wrinkles, and that make me think they are in their sixties.'
- 'I see her big ears, white hair and lots of wrinkles ,and that makes me think she is in her eighties.'

Use this technique until your child is able to hazard a guess that gets him close enough to the age. You are not looking for complete accuracy – leave that to those people who purport to be able to guess anyone's age! As long as he gets near the actual age, he will grow up knowing how to give relevant information or make pertinent comments and will be unlikely to say the wrong thing at the wrong time, for example 'How old are you, Mrs Brown?' or, to the head teacher, 'Your vest is showing'.

examples of boys who grow taller than their mum, but never become older than her. Or point out that his classmates grow at different rates but might be the same age, or perhaps siblings where a younger child is taller than the older one.

RELATIONSHIPS

Age becomes extremely important in knowing how to tell whether people are friends or family. Good communicators can tell very quickly, and subconsciously, whether someone is related or not.

I have found that an excellent way to teach this to children is to focus on whether the people they can see are the same age or different ages. I give them a 'rule' that tells them that if people are all the same age they are quite likely to be friends but if they are different ages they are more likely to be family. This may sound too easy, but it generally works.

Thus, knowing the approximate ages of people assists in determining relationships. Help your child to learn this simply by saying something like 'Look, those people are all different ages, so I think they are a family' or 'Those children are all the same age, so I think they are friends.' During my intervention, children pick this up really quickly. I then simply need to ask 'Are they the same

Family showing different ages
In a family not only are the children of different ages, the parents may be of different ages too.

age or different ages?' and the child will have a good idea whether they are friends or family.

You can also talk about the similarities in the look of siblings, but this is not always so helpful these days because of the number of step-siblings and adoptive siblings. The age comparison is generally more useful.

HOW WILL YOUR CHILD LEARN TO USE BODY LANGUAGE?
Emotional expression continues to develop as it did when your child was a baby. That is to say, his understanding of the levels of emotions comes before his ability to use them. So once he has learned to recognise different emotional states, the strength of feelings and the causes of these feelings in others, he can begin to apply the associated facial expressions and body language himself in similar circumstances.

Your child will only use body language and facial expressions that he has seen and learned. Notice how, just as he will experiment by copying simple words or gestures, he is also trying out and using the more sophisticated body language that

Firstly make sure your child knows what basic gestures mean. Test out 'pointing', for instance, and without saying anything point at an object or person and see if he understands that he needs to look where you are pointing.

Try getting ready to go out shopping without telling him this is what you are doing. Does he pick up that you are putting on your coat and gathering bags, money and keys together?

Body position, posture and direction of movement are the other indicators that you need to ensure your child is aware of. Take a look at the Introduction, page 18, to remind yourself about the significance of these aspects of body language. You can easily check your child's understanding by pointing out the stance and physical attitudes associated with different circumstances and emotions. Talk about what you see, ask your child what they think is happening, what people are feeling and why this might be so. Try to draw distinctions between different states, body positions and levels of tension, and so on.

Here are some examples: 'The woman is lying back in her chair. I think she is enjoying the sunshine. What do you think?' or 'The girl is concentrating so hard she is frowning,' or 'The boy is jumping up and down. What do you think he is feeling?' or 'Those children are queuing to go in the swimming pool. We need to stand behind them not in front of them'.

is associated with emotions. Encourage this every day if you can.

At first the body language should be exaggerated so that he can see it clearly and attempt to copy it. Gradually, as he becomes more skilled, he will notice the lower levels of expression that we use. As he learns to recognise a wider range of emotions and different levels of feeling, draw his attention to them by saying, for example, 'I am feeling a little bit confused now. Look at my face, I don't know which fruit to choose.'

You can still use nursery rhymes and action songs; they are an easy and fun way to encourage your child to develop the use of body language.

The simplest way to illustrate the notion of tension in the body is to think of the of the act of pointing at something or someone. Below are two examples to demonstrate this: even if we can't hear what is being said, the degree of tension in the body may

THE EFFECT OF TENSION

1. You want your child to look at the cat that is in the kitchen. So you say in a gentle but assertive manner 'Look at the cat'.
- At the same time you point your arm and index finger in the direction of the cat.
- The arm will be relaxed, slightly bent and definitely not stiff.

2. In another situation you want to point out the mess your child has made on the floor despite being told earlier to tidy it up.
- This time you will say 'Look at that mess!', but the voice will be different from the first example – there will be a brisk and slightly angry tone.
- There will also be a visible change in the pointing arm as it indicates the mess. It is now straight, stiff and tense.

give an important clue to what another person is feeling and the depth of that emotion.

If your child is unable to recognise such clues, he will be vulnerable in conflict situations and may find it very difficult to negotiate his way out. Help him feel the difference between tension and relaxation by getting him to hold your arm in different states of tension. Make sure he is looking at and feeling your arm while you explain what you are feeling.

TOUCH

When your child is coming up to school age, he needs to make further progress with understanding who it is acceptable to touch and who he should not touch. He also needs to learn how to touch appropriately, according to the person and the situation. It is important that his awareness is well developed before he enters school.

Touch ranges from cuddles and hugs early in life to situations where it may be right to hug another person who is not a family member. For example, if a another child hurts himself while playing, a toddler might show him sympathy and support with a hug.

Before school entry, children must begin to understand that hugging a teacher or dinner lady is not OK on an everyday basis and that hugging strangers is definitely out of the question. Again, this is all dependent on his ability to recognise and process the non-verbal information that tells him who is a close friend and who is a stranger.

Here are a few aspects concerning touch that you should draw to his attention:

1. The difference between acceptable and unacceptable kinds of touching — hugging, stroking, squeezing, pinching, hitting, biting etc.

2. Which parts of the body he can and can't touch — this might include pinching people's bottoms or sticking fingers in another child's ears!

3. Dangerous aspects of touching with fingers, hands, feet or legs — such as hitting or kicking, or touching his own or someone else's eyes.

Dad playing 'Look at my hands' with his daughter
Look how interested this little girl is in what her father is doing with his hands. She might even copy the movement next. She is learning about touch too.

4. Situational rules about touching different parts of his own body — for example it is not appropriate for him to touch his private parts in public.

He will only learn about touch if he sees acceptable touching within the family and if people talk about what these different ways of touching mean. Repeat as often as you can, so he really learns the meaning of touch and what it communicates.

Again, nursery rhymes and action songs can play a significant part in the development of this understanding because of all the movement, touching and repetition involved. Some examples are 'Incey Wincey spider', 'Ten in a bed', 'Knock at the door', 'Ten fat sausages', 'Heads, shoulders, knees and toes', 'The wheels on the bus', and so on. If your child is having a problem learning to use touch appropriately, make up rhymes where different types of touch are involved, for example gentle stroking, tickling, loving and so on.

Obviously, if your child doesn't develop a good understanding of how to touch appropriately, then others will be surprised or taken aback by his inappropriate touching, and his life at school will be problematic.

PROXIMITY AND PERSONAL SPACE

Proximity means knowing how close to get to people. Because they help you interpret relationships and situations, all the skills that we have looked at up to now will contribute to your child's ability to correctly apply awareness of proximity.

This is something that is also culturally related and becomes more and more sensitive the older your child becomes. Therefore it is important to give your child the awareness and skill that he can build on so that in his teens he will know how close to get with regard to members of the opposite sex.

TRY THIS!

Play rubbing noses as in the Maori or Inuit greeting. Contrast this with pinching his nose using the nursery rhyme 'Sing a song of sixpence', which ends with:

'The maid was in the garden hanging out the clothes when down came a blackbird and pecked off her nose' (pretend you have taken his nose with your thumb poking out between your first and second fingers.)

Talk about the contrasting feeling between the gentle rub and the pinch.

He learns how close to stand to people when he is communicating with them partly by experiencing, and talking about, a variety of situations and partly from observing other people and how close they stand to one another. So when your child stands too close to you, say 'I don't want you to stand so close to me' (or words to that effect). When he moves, you will need to say something like 'That's right' to confirm that the distance he chooses is suitable. In this way he will develop a 'rule' that tells him how close to stand when talking to you. If you don't do this, he may stand too close again and develop an unsuitable 'rule'. If you don't comment, he will simply do what he thinks is right regardless of what is socially acceptable.

Before he goes to school he will need to have developed a high level of understanding about the different rules that relate to how close to stand when talking to family and friends, teachers,

so close. I want you to stand there,' and indicate where with your hand. If he shows signs of not learning the rule, repeat this phrase so he has more chance of replicating the behaviour you want him to use.

MAKING SENSE OF SITUATIONS

As we saw in the previous chapter, interpreting what is happening in situations is very important. Your child now needs to learn to distinguish between clues that are relevant and helpful in any given situation and those that he can ignore. Throughout his toddler years, you should help him to focus on the meaningful signs that aid his 'reading' of a situation.

Draw his attention to the clues that confirm your understanding of a situation. Fancy curtains and a sofa, for example, indicate a living room. Ignore the unhelpful clues such as pot plants, which might make him think he is in a garden centre. This is not as silly as it sounds — many older children pick up the wrong signal and form a completely different idea of where they are.

Your child will need to learn how to recognise situations from small but relevant clues. For instance 'taps and a basin' signify a bathroom whereas 'taps and a sink' signify a kitchen. Before he starts school, he must be able to focus on these important clues and ignore those that may detract from a good understanding of the situation.

Now that he knows who people are and what kind of situation they are in, he needs to draw a conclusion about what they are doing. This is so much easier if he has correctly identified the first two pieces of information. If he doesn't do all this in the correct order, he may leap to the wrong conclusion about what they are doing. Sometimes he will be right, but mostly he will get it wrong and end up talking about, or doing something, at odds with the situation and the people present.

Not being able to tell that he is in the school hall for gym rather than for assembly will put him at a disadvantage. At a pre-school age his misunderstanding of situations might appear 'cute', but by the time he is six or seven this behaviour will cause him problems and will be much harder

Proximity
We can see these people know each other exceptionally well because of how close they are to one another. Your child will pick up such clues by seeing many different examples of couples, brothers and sisters and acquaintances.

strangers and so on. Talk about proximity in a variety of circumstances, for example parents and their children, adults with other people's children, adults with strangers, doctors with patients, teachers with their classes.

You should never assume, when you tell your child not to do something, that he knows what rule he should be using for this particular situation. (I once saw a 13-year-old place himself directly between me and his teacher while we were talking. With his back to me, he began talking to the teacher and fiddling with the teacher's tie!) It is always best if you say, 'I don't want you to stand

for you to change. Taking this opportunity now to check that he knows what situational clues are, and what they mean, will help to prevent problems once he is at school.

MAKING CONNECTIONS

Your child's behaviour is directly related to his ability to understand what is going on and to communicate effectively what he wants to do. Between the ages of two and four he is likely to be unable to take in everything that is being said to him because his understanding of spoken language will not be sufficient to process all the words in a sentence. When we listen to people speaking, we focus on the words that have particular value in helping us access meaning. We pay less attention to words whose purpose is mainly grammatical.

In the same way, when we encounter a scene or situation we focus on the non-verbal clues that

WHAT CAN HAPPEN?

The Stuarts didn't think their child had a problem because most of the time he appeared to understand what was happening in situations. What he told them seemed to make sense, so they hadn't wondered how he had drawn the conclusion.

However, when Billy was five, he went with his mum to the hospital for an appointment. The nurses had put a lot of flowers in the waiting room. For the next appointment, Billy went to the hospital with his Dad. Mrs Stuart was shocked to be told that Billy thought they had gone to buy some flowers.

Because Billy had looked at the flowers rather than the nurses' uniforms and the ill people, he drew the wrong conclusion. His mother just found this 'funny', and she didn't check whether he had been using relevant clues to interpret other situations. Billy found it harder and harder to generalise his understanding of situations, and when he started school he began to find all the new and unfamiliar situations very difficult to understand.

The Williams family, on the other hand, always asked their child how he knew what people were doing in this manner:

Mrs Williams: *'What do you think those children are doing, Timmy?'*
Timmy: *'They are going ice skating.'*
Mrs Williams: *'What makes you think that?'*
Timmy: *'Because they are selling ice-creams.'*

Timmy got the first answer right, but for the wrong reasons. He had focused on clues that were not directly pertinent. However, his parents had an opportunity to redirect his understanding to the relevant clues. This meant that in future situations Timmy would focus on the skates and the ice rink, ignoring the ice-creams, and as a result would make a good interpretation of what was happening.

I have assessed many children, of all ages, and it is astonishing how many school-aged children – both primary and secondary – could not identify in a photo that two adults and a child were sitting in a doctor's waiting room, waiting to see the doctor. The children mostly thought the people were at home and, when asked what made them think this, the response was 'Because there is a carpet and a radiator'. Their interpretation was based on looking at the wrong clues, despite there being other more relevant indicators.

help us understand meaning and significance and we filter out things that are simply part of the 'background noise'. This is a more challenging task as there is so much more information from which to select.

New situations or ones that your child doesn't encounter every day may be particularly challenging. This is partly because his language skills are not sufficiently developed but mostly because his interpretation of the non-verbal information is limited. Being able to look at the relevant things in a situation is key to making good sense of what is happening and to predicting what may happen next.

If your child has not looked at people sufficiently between birth and beginning school entry, he will not have enough information in his 'database' to be able to compare and contrast situations and then make the appropriate deductions and connections.

To overcome this, make sure your child's interpretational skills are developing well and that he is able to make good sense of both simple and complex situations. Help him notice when things look similar but are slightly different. Talk about the differences. It is never too late to do this and you will be surprised how he changes.

HIDDEN MEANINGS
This refers to phrases where words alone don't carry the message, for example 'Pull your socks up!' or 'I am pulling your leg' or 'He's over the hill'. To understand the message, you need to look at the contextual

clues to tell you whether or not to process the words 'literally'. For example, if someone's socks were falling down, the message 'Pull your socks up' would make literal sense. If not, another interpretation is necessary. Imagine what you would make of phrases like 'get stuck in' or 'go up in smoke' or 'falling out with someone' if you couldn't see beyond the literal meaning of the words.

Most people know that children who have either an autistic or an Asperger's diagnosis find understanding hidden meanings very hard. They tend to interpret things at face value. This can be amusing when the child is at pre-school or in the early years of primary school, but later it becomes a serious impediment to understanding the world.

To acquire understanding of hidden meanings, your child needs to have excellent non-verbal processing skills. Then he will look at the clues telling him about the context and will associate these with past experiences. If he is processing all this effectively, he will be more likely to understand when the meaning is literal and when it is not.

Autistic spectrum children who have benefited from the Not Just Talking intervention programme are able to understand and communicate

Situational information
We know this girl is going on a beach holiday in this country and probably for more than a week because of the number of suitcases, the dog, the beach ball, the rubber ring and the mat! We can also assume the family is not going abroad because the dog wouldn't be travelling on a plane!

effectively about hidden meanings because their non-verbal interpretation improves significantly.

INNUENDO
Innuendo requires us to understand that an oblique rather than a direct suggestion is being made. As you will now appreciate, your child's recognition of innuendo depends on good non-verbal processing of complex information. For example, 'Wouldn't it be nice if the door was shut?' is an indirect way of asking the listener to shut the door. 'You are not made of glass,' when someone is blocking your view of the TV, may be seen as a less aggressive way of saying 'Get out of the way'.

HUMOUR AND SARCASM
Hidden meanings are central to humour, and most verbal jokes are based on the listener's skill in not taking things literally, for example 'What kind of pie can fly?' ... 'A magpie'. Or 'How many elephants can you get in a mini?' ... 'Two in the front and two in the back'. Also, there are often subtle connections that have to be made in order to understand a joke. Puns, in particular, are based on recognising double meanings.

Children who are unable to process this level of subtlety prefer visual humour, which does not depend on contextual understanding or hidden meanings. Examples are Mr Bean or Charlie Chaplin and other language-free, humorous cartoons, films or theatre.

You can have fun with verbal humour. Start with simple jokes that don't need much understanding of other things and can be easily demonstrated, such as 'Why does a flamingo lift one leg?' ... 'Because if it lifted both it would fall over!'

When sarcasm is used, the level of complexity shifts up a gear or two! The problem for children is that the facial expression and body language are usually communicating different messages. To compound this, the message is also not understood by simply listening to the words .

Telling someone they are 'such a genius' when the situation clearly communicates that this person is anything but a genius, needs the listener to recognise that tone of voice and facial expression

WHAT CAN HAPPEN?

The difficulty for children, particularly when they enter secondary school, is that sarcasm is sometimes used by teachers to control children or communicate disapproval to a child who is not behaving in a suitable manner. For example:

1. John has failed to develop the ability to process non-verbal information and, therefore, may miss the initial, low-level signs that tell him his teacher is unhappy about something.

2. Rather than get angry and shout, his teacher uses oblique facial expressions and body language to express her displeasure, adding: 'Well, what a surprise! John is finally listening.'

3. The stress and intonation will change – certain words may be exaggerated and the intonation will be lively. If the intention was directly expressed by the words, there would not be a great need for emphasis.

4. The actual message – that John isn't paying attention – is hidden behind what is being said and this is very confusing for him.

5. As the child failed to notice his teacher's initial, simpler non-verbal expression of displeasure, he will have little chance of understanding the hidden message in her sarcasm.

6. Your child may come into conflict with teachers who assume that a child who talks well is simply choosing to be naughty, or behave oddly, and fail to understand that he may be having problems interpreting commonplace non-verbal clues.

are changing the meaning of the words. For instance, when something has gone wrong, saying 'Oh great, that's just what I need', with a face expressing dejection and a falling intonation, conveys exactly the opposite of the literal meaning of the words. We often use sarcasm to soften a difficult message.

The common thread to all these hidden meanings is that, to understand them, the listener must have good interpretational skills. Being able to appreciate hidden meanings enriches your child's life because he will understand more of what is going on round him and can have fun with language.

FOCUS POINTS

★ Encourage your child to develop interest in, and make use of, all aspects of non-verbal interpretation.

★ Talk about what bodies communicate.

★ Identify the signs of gender.

★ Talk about the obvious indicators of age.

★ Help him notice what clothes communicate and how different ways of wearing them can change the meaning.

★ Comment on how to know whether children and other people are friends or family.

★ Continue to do nursery rhymes, lap games and action songs with your child, encouraging his use of body language through the exaggerated actions.

★ Does he recognise and use day-to-day gestures such as waving goodbye, pointing or shrugging the shoulders?

★ Introduce activities where he experiences different types of touching.

★ Talk about appropriate and inappropriate touching seen in others – don't forget to tell him what should be happening.

★ Help him feel the difference between tension and relaxation in your body and recognise the difference from just seeing it.

★ Ensure that your child understands proximity by giving very clear verbal and visual signals about what is acceptable and what is not. Point out where others stand in relation to the person they are talking to.

★ This technique can also be used for all kinds of situations where your child needs to learn rules, such as 'I don't want you to talk to me when I am on the phone. Wait until I have finished.'

★ Talk about the signs that tell you what situation you are in, for example 'There are rows of desks, so this must be a classroom' or 'Look at the trolleys – we're going into the supermarket.'

★ Be explicit when using hidden meanings. If you say something like 'I am going to put my feet up', also tell him what those words actually mean.

★ Have fun with verbal humour – help him to understand the hidden meanings.

★ Don't expect him to learn any of these skills from the TV. He has to see them in real life.

KNOWING WHAT YOU FEEL

In this chapter you will see the progress in emotional understanding that your child now needs to make if she is to be able to communicate her own feelings effectively. She will need plenty of practice to translate her understanding of other people's emotions before she can convey her own — through facial expressions and body language, as well as words. If she is unable to do this, she will find it very hard to relate to others' feelings or express her own in an appropriate way — two essential life skills.

WHAT DO MUMMY AND DADDY FEEL?

As we saw when we looked at the development of these skills during the very early years, getting your baby interested in faces is a vital step towards her understanding the emotions indicated by different facial expressions. A child is born into the world not knowing anything about how people feel. She has to learn this, bit by bit, from what she sees going on around her.

A baby's level of emotional understanding is quite basic, recognising only simple, clear or vivid emotional states. Now that your child is learning to talk, understanding has to make a huge leap forward. As a toddler, she is starting to become a confident walker, able to explore her environment. She encounters new situations and people; everything is more varied, facial expressions included.

Expression of feeling

This girl wants some sweets and her mother doesn't want her to have them. Because the girl is watching the mother's face so intently, she is picking up the level of disapproval being expressed. Also the girl is able to use a complex facial expression to communicate her frustration and anger at not being allowed to do what she wants.

Expressions are not larger than life, however, and more attention to people's faces is required. She will need a lot of help from others to develop her awareness of the clues. As her parents, you need to help her to learn what to look at and what to ignore in what she sees around her. You can also encourage other 'competent' communicators, such as grandparents or brothers and sisters, to do the same. Everybody needs to help your child develop the understanding and skills that make it easier for her to communicate.

For instance, once your child is able to recognise expressions such as 'happy' and 'angry', she can learn the reasons why you might have these feelings. It is not sufficient for her to notice and learn the facial expressions and body language; she must also know why you are feeling 'happy' or 'angry'. Help her to do this by saying (and signing) 'It's sunny, I feel happy,' or 'Uh oh! Trouble! I broke the cup!'

You know how important it is to interest your child in looking at people talking and now you will need to develop this interest by asking her about what people might be saying, thinking, feeling and doing. Seeing her maintain her interest in increasingly complex or changing facial expressions will help you realise that she has made this big step in her communication development. If she can do this, she will be better equipped to recognise the facial expressions of her teacher when she starts school and will adjust more readily to new situations, allowing her to get the best out of her education.

HOW TO HELP HER
It is only when looking at you that your child will associate the facial expressions with the emotion. When she sees new emotions, such as 'bored' or 'upset', exaggerate them temporarily, so she picks up the clues easily. Once she is really skilled at identifying new emotions, you can moderate the expressions, but when introducing her to new emotions, make things as clear as you can for her. Assuming that your child is now fully aware of basic feelings such as 'happy', 'sad', 'angry', 'bored', 'like', 'dislike', 'love', 'surprised',

'worried', and so on, you can move on to the more complex emotions described on page 86. However, you must be sure that she knows these basic ones, most of which are covered in Margaret Miller's *Baby Faces* book.

COMPLEX INTERPRETATION
Now that she is able to know 'who' is in the situation, 'where' they are and 'what' they are doing, you can begin to help her know what the people might be thinking, saying and feeling.

If she is still not correctly interpreting clues relating to the situation and/or the people in it, she is unlikely to know what people might be thinking, feeling or saying. When you see two or more people talking, help her by asking the following questions:

1. What are they talking about?
2. What might they be thinking?
3. What are they going to do next?
4. What are they feeling?

Only if the listener makes a reply that is relevant to the topic will the speaker know they are listening. If she is unable to answer any of these, you must tell her what you think, for example:

1. I see them looking into shopping bags so I think they are talking about what they have bought.

2. That girl is looking into the toy shop. Look at her face. She wants a toy. Perhaps she thinks her Mummy will buy it for her.

3. They have bikes and are wearing cycle helmets. I think they are going for a cycle ride. They look happy because they like riding their bikes.

4. That boy is holding his arm and has a sad face. I see he has fallen off his bike. I think he is crying because he has hurt his arm.

Talking about these things with your child gives her opportunities to hear what you think. Don't assume she sees the world in the same way as you.

WHICH EMOTIONS SHOULD I SHOW HER?

Many parents believe children should be kept from strong emotions such as anger because they think young children should only experience positive emotions. It is very important that she learns both positive and negative feelings. If she doesn't, she will have limited understanding later in life. The home is the most supportive place to learn about difficult emotions. You don't want her having to learn about them with people she doesn't know well.

Nursery rhymes, as well as fairy tales and books about monsters, are central to storytelling

TRY THIS!

Here are a few suggestions of complex emotions that you can introduce to your child, either through looking at people in real situations or when reading stories, picking up the visual differences between opposite emotions where appropriate:

- Happy and excited – emphasise the difference between these two. It is mostly to do with level and cause. For example, you are happy to be asked to a party and excited about going.
- 'Friendly' and 'unfriendly'
- 'Kind' and 'unkind'
- 'Frightened' or 'scared' – focus on the use of only one of these words to start with; be consistent.
- 'Jealous' – it is easy to talk about this if your child has brothers or sisters, but if not, find it in a story, preferably with pictures of real people feeling jealous, and try to relate it to situations that she comes across; or use toy animals to role play this.
- 'Lonely' – an important emotion to help your child learn early on in a non-threatening way. Play games with her toys and have a situation where her teddy, for example, is left on his own. Always resolve the situation by suggesting what teddy could do to stop feeling lonely.
- 'Pleased with' what she has done or others have done – this should be developed before 'proud', which can have negative connotations. But just being 'pleased with' yourself is simpler as it relates to everyday activities. 'Proud' is reserved for special circumstances. Also you can be a little 'pleased' or very 'pleased', for instance say 'I am pleased with the tidying up' or 'I am very pleased you have eaten your dinner'. When she has done something you think she might be pleased about, ask her: 'Do you feel pleased with your painting?'
- 'Hurt' – this can be physical or emotional. I would start with physical examples: if you see her doing something that might have hurt her, say what she has done and ask whether she hurt herself.
- 'Interested' and 'uninterested' – really important for good conversations. Whenever the occasion arises, point out faces of people who are 'interested' in books or pictures or a conversation, as well as people who are showing signs of being uninterested or bored. Talk about your child when she shows boredom or interest too.
- Being 'focused' or 'paying attention' – it is important to be able to demonstrate these states. If she is focused but doesn't look it when she is at school, her teacher won't know that she is concentrating. NB there is a difference between focusing on your work and paying attention to a teacher.

for children. They allow you to show your child negative emotions in a safe setting, that is, through pretend or 'make believe' — in itself an important communication skill to develop in your child. I have worked with many teenagers who had still not developed a full understanding about the difference between fantasy and reality. (See 'Related skills', page 121, for more on this.)

Helping your child to learn both positive and negative emotions and to understand what 'pretend' means can be achieved so simply from an early age by using the phrase 'Let's pretend' whenever you are doing something like having a tea party or making a toilet roll into a train.

Even if your child doesn't know what a word means, as long as it is repeated often enough and she is looking at the situation, she will come to understand it. You can use this method to help her learn difficult and new words in many other situations, the basic principle being to say the word enough times and relate it to specific situations or objects — as long as she is looking at them. The more you comment on what she might be feeling and what might have caused the feeling, the sooner she will be able to recognise it for herself.

SHE HAS FEELINGS TOO

Once your child has been able to recognise your non-verbal communication of feelings, and can associate them with the cause of those feelings, she will be able to connect this with what she herself feels when similar events happen to her. For example, she sees you become 'happy' when you have an ice-cream because you like them and you label the feeling as 'happy' and you tell her what has caused you to feel this way.

So when she has an ice-cream and she feels a nice feeling inside, she will start to recognise that this is 'happiness', especially if you point out that she looks 'happy'. The more situations in which she sees people express their emotions and talk about the different causes, the more likely she is to be able to recognise and name her own feelings.

It sounds like a long process, but if you do this routinely, through her everyday experiences, she will accumulate all that she needs to make good sense of all the emotions she sees.

DIFFERENT LEVELS OF EMOTIONAL UNDERSTANDING

Next, it is important for her to notice variations in the intensity of feeling, for example when you are a little bit happy or sad. This is communicated in a more subtle way, so you will need to signal these less obvious expressions very clearly. As an adult you might express the different levels of emotion associated with being 'cross' as 'irritated', 'cross', 'angry' and 'furious'. Your child doesn't need to know these words at this stage; she just needs to understand that there are different levels of feeling. She needs to relate the high-level emotions that you have already taught her to these low-level, less obvious emotions.

Draw your child's attention to this low-level non-verbal communication as it happens. When she kicks the chair, for example, tell her what you are feeling: 'Kicking the chair is making me a little bit angry'. Encourage her to look at your face and, if necessary, draw her attention to your stern voice or the fact that you are frowning, not smiling.

Ensure that your tone of voice and body language are in harmony. Being able to decide

How angry am I?
This man is quite a bit angry. Children need to pick up the frown, the eyes, the mouth and the tense hand pointing aggressively. They will then understand the level of anger and know how to react and not make him any angrier.

which emotion to concentrate on when the face and body language are saying different things is a very high-level skill that normally develops from four or five. For more about conflicting messages from faces and bodies, see sarcasm and hidden meanings in 'Hidden meanings', page 81.

Once she is aware of high- and low-level emotions, your child needs to learn to recognise emotions at a mid-level, for example a face that is content or satisfied rather than just exaggeratedly happy. Because the clues are less clear cut, she will have to be more attentive to faces, even when she is not involved in the conversation. These times are as important as one-to-one interactions because she will be seeing two (or more) people making normal, everyday expressions that she can relate to other, similar experiences.

Your aim is that she should recognise the lowest levels of common emotional states and be able to adjust her behaviour accordingly, to her benefit. For example, if she sees her daddy getting a little angry with her, she can do what he wants to stop him from becoming even more angry.

HOW TO IDENTIFY FEELINGS IN OTHERS
Not only does she need to recognise different facial expressions in her parents, carers and siblings, but she also has to recognise the same expressions in other people with whom she is less familiar.

We all communicate through facial expressions in a similar but slightly different manner. So, for example, a child must learn to notice that when Mrs Brown, the neighbour, is moderately happy, she shows it in a similar manner to Mummy, that is, she has a little smile and her eyes widen a bit but, unlike Mummy, she doesn't nod her head at the same time.

Apply this simple example to other situations and the importance of recognising similarities and differences will become clear. Here are some examples of people who communicate irritation (low-level anger) in slightly different ways:

- Father: frowns and at the same time looks a bit quizzical. He may also raise a hand with a pointed finger. He uses a sing-song, slightly sarcastic, stern voice.

- Mother: frowns but purses her lips; her body tenses a little and she puts her hands on her hips.
- Teacher in primary school: frowns a bit, makes her voice deeper and more formal, and her body becomes straight; she folds her arms and looks disapprovingly at the individual or group causing the problem.
- Friends: may show irritation in a variety of ways, such as stamping, throwing things, walking away. Some may have non-verbal communication problems and therefore show irritation at a very high level or in an idiosyncratic manner.
- Teachers in secondary school: here, the problem is exacerbated because in any one day, the child has to make sense of a number of different teachers, all of whom will have slightly different ways of communicating low-level anger.

The variations above could be very confusing to a child who has not developed the ability to recognise similarities and differences in a variety of emotional expressions or levels of feeling. There is a huge shift between primary and secondary school in the numbers of faces your child will have to look at and understand — cumulatively it could reach more than ten teachers

Looking at feelings
This little girl is looking intently at close quarters at her grandmother's face, which is communicating that the girl needs to be quiet.

WHAT MUST YOUR CHILD BE ABLE TO DO?

Here is a summary of how your child needs to learn about emotions:

1. She sees basic emotions at a very high level.

2. Because she has become keen to look at people, she will see at the same time what might have caused the emotion. For example: Dad gave Mum a hug – which made Mum smile; or another child dropped a plate or continued to throw the ball in the house – which made Mum cross.

3. She hears comments on the cause and the emotion, for example 'Thank you for hugging me. Hugging makes me feel very happy' and sees you smiling.

4. Your child makes a connection between the cause, the facial expression and the emotion.

5. When she experiences a similar situation and feels something that reminds her of the emotion that she saw her parents feeling, she can start to recognise that her own emotion will match what she has seen and heard. She will then experiment with using non-verbal methods of communicating these feelings. If these are interpreted well by others, she will continue to 'try out' these new emotions in other situations.

6. The more she experiences these feelings, especially with different people demonstrating them, the easier it will be to learn to recognise, interpret and express them.

7. Gradually, as she becomes more aware, she starts to notice the subtle gradations of emotion. But this takes time, so please be patient.

8. She should become competent at recognising varying levels of emotion by about four or five years of age – but definitely before she starts school.

per week, plus the head teacher, deputy, head of tutorial group, SENCO, dinner staff, and so on.

The inability to recognise facial expressions in different people is one explanation (alongside other social and educational pressures on children at secondary school) for the high referral rate to Not Just Talking of children in their first and second year at secondary school. Children who have managed to survive the one-teacher system at primary school suddenly have to cope with many more teachers and, therefore, many more faces, all communicating in subtly different ways from each other.

It is much better to develop these skills while your child is a toddler; children who don't, and therefore can't process non-verbal information as described here, become vulnerable as teenagers because they can't respond appropriately to clues warning them of trouble. This is why it is vital that, having learned to recognise basic emotions, your child develops the awareness that people communicate similar emotions in ways that might be a bit different but mean the same thing. Then she needs to be able to compare and differentiate in order to interpret accurately.

By the time your child starts at school, she should, at the very least, be able to identify low-, mid- and high-level emotional communication for more than ten emotions – happy, angry, bored, loving, sad, surprised and so on. Different children may learn different emotions, or call them something else; that doesn't matter. As long as your child understands and uses a number and range of emotions, and recognises at least three levels of feeling – positive and negative – she should find the transition to school relatively smooth.

WHO AM I?

Conversations start from the basis that one person is sufficiently interested in the other to share what they know with them or ask for information. This skill grows from those early attempts to get your baby interested in faces. He learns that people are interesting and do unusual things that are worth enquiring about.

We saw that babies start to distinguish between family and people who are strangers at the age of about six to eight months. This is one of the first indications you will get that your child knows that people are separate individuals. But there is a great deal more development he needs to undergo in order to recognise the difference between close friends, people he sees less often, new people introduced by you and those who are complete strangers.

Give your child daily opportunities either to participate in or to watch conversations about what is going on in his life. The more you tell him what you are thinking and the more you ask him questions about what he is thinking, the more he will learn about the differences between your thoughts and his and the more he will want to communicate as a result.

SELF-AWARENESS

Unless he learns that he is a distinct and separate individual, your child will not learn that other people's minds contain different knowledge, levels of information, experiences and feelings. So you need to help him learn that other people are separate and distinct beings. Without this understanding, there may be no reason to talk to people. After all, if he thinks that everyone else has the same thoughts as him, what would be the point of him learning something as difficult as communication? It would be easier to treat other people as objects.

It is my opinion that developing the skill of knowing that others think different thoughts is central to our ability to communicate. Others working in this field might say that failure to do this is a symptom of autism. However, in my

TRY THIS!

'Look at me!' – a game to help your son notice changes in you

- Collect a box of funny hats, earrings, stick-on shapes, brooches, scarves, tinsel, large and colourful spectacles – anything that will make a difference to your appearance.
- Start by facing each other.
- Then turn your back on him and choose something big and noticeable from the box and put it on or around your head. This will also draw his attention to your face – a very useful bonus of this game.
- Turn round to face him, saying something that tells him you are about to turn round, such as 'Here I come' or 'Now look at me!', then add 'What is different?'
- See if he notices what has changed. Help him if he doesn't by saying something like 'Is it on my face?', 'Is it on my arm?', gradually moving his attention towards the part of your body where he will find it.
- You want him to notice for himself, so only tell him if you think he is not going to see it after two or three clues.
- When you do point out the difference, make what you say large and noticeable, like 'There it is! – I have a big red ball hanging from my ear!'
- Make the changes very noticeable to start with, but gradually aim to reduce their size to something very small such as a star or a ring on your finger.
- Give him a go too! But don't spot the difference too soon.
- Make it fun!

experience, you can promote understanding in most children of what other people may know or feel and, when you do that, they are often no longer viewed as autistic.

A child who doesn't have the ability to tell the difference between himself and others will:

- be unable to give good information
- assume that other people have seen what he has seen
- talk to others as if they have intimate knowledge of his life and experiences
- make communication difficult for others who attempt to hold a conversation with him
- be unable to make and keep friends.

So please help your child learn how to do this. You will be giving him a better future.

INTEREST IN OTHERS
Interest in people needs to grow during these toddler years. Encourage this interest by helping your child to participate in different activities, such as reading books and playing games, in different social settings — playgroups, mother and toddler groups, childminder settings, parties, other family homes, and so on. The more he becomes keen to make contact with other people, the more likely it is that others will want to communicate with him. He will develop good communication skills through experiences where

Interest in others
This little boy is developing his communication well by being so interested in what his mum is doing. Also, they are making pastry, which will be outside his daily experiences and a wonderful activity for him to join in.

he is watching others communicating in different situations. It will develop his vocabulary, too. Your child's ability to recognise similarities and differences in people's faces and what emotions they are expressing now needs to deepen and expand so that he develops a real understanding of the children in his friendship group as distinct from strangers. Point out these differences as often as possible.

As he grows older, your little boy will ask you about things that he doesn't know, for example 'Where Grandma gone?' This is a sign that he recognises different people. Or he tells you something you don't know: if he sees a bird in the garden and you have been busy looking at something else, he may say 'Saw bird'.

Because he talks about things you haven't seen or experienced, you will know that he understands that you don't have the same information in your head as him. Messages like 'Where has Grandma gone?' and 'I saw a bird in the garden' also tell you that your child is developing 'theory of mind'.

As he gets past about two years of age, this type of information giving and requesting should increase day by day. If your child is not doing both these things, you really need to focus on the skills that precede these, as described in 'Knowing me, knowing you', page 48. If your child has sufficient

WHAT IS 'THEORY OF MIND'?

Theory of mind is the ability we have to see the world from another person's point of view. Most professionals understand that this develops in the first year of a child's life, but they may not relate it to the development in his interpretational skills. I believe that:

- theory of mind is a crucial part of communication itself
- the failure to develop it is not only found in autism
- it is possible to develop this skill in many children who show signs of lacking it.

At this toddler stage, however, you just need to ensure you are always commenting about what you are thinking or what others might be thinking: 'I am feeling really tired because I have worked hard cleaning the car' or 'That man is asking his wife what she wants to eat'. Ask your child questions such as: 'What is that boy doing? Why is he doing it?'; 'What are those children talking about?'; 'What are those children going to do?' Anything that gets your child to put himself in someone else's shoes and see the world from their perspective will help establish these skills. Encouraging this from an early age will help him accumulate the understanding required for everyday communication.

If he is unable to put himself in the shoes of another person and know what they might be feeling or thinking, your child will not know what to say to people. He will assume that his thoughts and those of others are the same and therefore that he has no need to communicate. Our drive to communicate happens when we know that what is in our brain is different from someone else's.

The reason why the Not Just Talking intervention programme is so successful in producing theory of mind in children is because the child learns how to recognise what people are feeling from body language and facial expressions, and the therapy relates this improved understanding to what might happen and what the child might say in response to different emotional states.

skills relating to 'Knowing you, knowing me', then there is no reason why he won't develop this higher level of understanding, as long as you give him the chance. There is more about information giving in 'Making conversations work', page 96.

As we have seen, mirrors are a helpful way of gaining interest in self and others. You could develop the idea of copying actions that he sees in the mirror. Introduce face painting and dressing up in extraordinary wigs, earrings, glasses and hats – anything that helps him to be interested in and want to copy what he sees. See Jackie Cooke's book, *Early Sensory Skills*, on activities and ideas for establishing all kinds of early skills relating to this and other areas of non-verbal skill development.

UNDERSTANDING FAMILY RELATIONSHIPS

The key here is that your child is able to understand that individuals can have relationships with people other than himself and that this need not affect their relationship with him. For instance, you still love him, even when you hug his brother or sister.

To start with, your child has to develop relationships with both his father and his mother. Their roles are very different: put simply, the mother's role is to give the child love and attention and the father's role is to help the child understand that he is able to have loving relationships with others but they will be different. Of course, there is a cross-over between the two and they are equally important and meaningful in a child's development.

The father's role is especially important because without it the child can become over-dependent on his mother and may not learn how to communicate effectively with others. Both roles can be achieved in same-sex partnerships too; the basic concept is that there are two people reacting in loving but different ways, giving different skills to the child.

In single-parent families where there is no other person living in the home with whom the child can develop a relationship that is not the 'mothering' relationship, the child will not find it easy to relate to other people. This can be overcome by ensuring that he has regular contact with a significant other, such as a grandmother or an uncle, who has a different type of relationship with him from that

of the person in the mothering role. It won't work if this second person mothers him too. The second person's role is to help the child develop this key aspect of his communication skills, rather than replicating the mothering role. As the child grows older, this relationship becomes equally valued.

So he learns from the non-verbal clues what his relationship with his mother is and how it differs from that with his father. He should also start to appreciate that your love for him is constant and, although at times you might be angry with him, this underlying relationship is not affected.

Children who are singletons (the only child) may also find this hard because they are unable to develop the skills associated with sharing their parents with siblings. But, as with all these 'problem' areas for non-verbal communication development, it is a question of awareness; as long as you are aware of the importance of exposure to different relationships, then your child will develop the ability to function in different situations.

FRIENDS AND STRANGERS

Your child will need to recognise who he knows and who is new to him. Gradually, as your child recognises the difference between family and strangers, he may start to appear 'shy'. This is a good sign that he really understands the difference. By the time he is four or five he has to be able to tell that some people are friends but others are not. Introduce quite early the concept of family, friends and people you don't know.

To introduce the idea to your child, just point out people at a distance that you have never met. Whenever you are out shopping or in the park, make it clear to him which people you know and which you don't, saying something like 'I am not talking to that man because I don't know him, he is a stranger.' Keep it simple, as obviously there will be some occasions when you do talk to strangers.

SHARED KNOWLEDGE

Your child will also need to know the level of detail that is pertinent to give to different people in different circumstances. Being able to recognise when someone is not known to the family also

TRY THIS!

Here are some ideas to encourage your child's interest in communication.

- A photo album or scrapbook of your child growing up from birth is an excellent way of helping him develop a sense of himself.
- Take photos of him doing different things, for example having his breakfast, seeing his grandad, walking the dog, having a bath.
- Add pictures of you and any of his brothers or sisters doing similar things.
- Talk about the similarities and differences between one person and another.
- Show these people at different ages too, doing both the same and different sorts of things.
- Expand on this by adding friends and other more distant members of his family.
- Introduce the concept of strangers – say something like 'We don't know those people in the shop. We have never seen them before. They are strangers.'
- To make it bit more challenging, add what people might be saying, thinking or feeling.
- Talk about what might happen next from the clues in the photos.
- You could also comment on other members of the family or friends who do things differently from your child, for example he might eat with a spoon but Daddy eats with a knife and fork.
- Elaborate about the information we usually leave out. For instance, instead of saying 'Let's go now', try 'Look – we have all got our coats on and we have the car keys and shopping bags, so we are going to the supermarket **now**.'
- Ask him about something that you don't know, such what he has been doing at playgroup or nursery. Help him to give you the right level of detail so that you understand what he is saying, for example 'I don't know John. Who is he?'
- Identify people from an early stage as either 'family', 'friends' or 'strangers'.
- When you are out, talk about the people you see and know, and those you don't know.
- Gradually introduce the idea that he does not talk to strangers unless you are there.
- Point out that when you are telling him about something you do regularly, you don't need to be so specific.

makes it easier later on to talk about what you might discuss within the family and what is acceptable to tell others. He will only know this if he understands the idea of 'shared knowledge'.

A child who doesn't know what is appropriate information to give is likely to go up to total strangers and tell them intimate details about his family life, or he may ask other people unsuitable questions despite having been told many times not to, such as asking the vicar what colour pants his wife wears!

'Shared knowledge' refers to the experiences and information that we share with other people.

This knowledge is often greatest among family members, for example everybody knows that Saturday morning is when the family goes to swimming lessons. So, when talking about this sort of event, your family will not need to be as clear and specific as when your child tells his teacher about it, because his teacher's shared knowledge of the home-based activity would be minimal.

At home you might say at breakfast on a Saturday 'Are we going today?' Because there is 'shared knowledge' that swimming happens every Saturday, you can use a kind of shorthand. However, if your child wants to tell his teacher when he goes

Fun in the pool
This girl is having great fun in the swimming pool. When she has finished she will have lots to say to her friends and family about what she did in the pool today.

to school on Monday, he will have to be much more specific and say, 'On Saturday I went for my swimming lesson. It was great fun.' If he used only the level of detail he would use at home, his teacher would have no idea what he was talking about.

Having an understanding of the knowledge shared with the person with whom you are communicating helps you determine how much and what information to give them. A child who doesn't know about shared knowledge will talk as

if the person he is speaking to knows everything he knows, so will use a shorthand form that won't make sense to his listener. Children with conversational skill problems who are referred to me for assessment often talk to me as though I have been in the playground with them and know the children they refer to, or they will talk about a children's programme on TV assuming that I have seen it too.

This is an indication that they think I have the same knowledge about events as they do. We all have slightly or even very different understanding, depending on our experiences or our perception of the experiences that we share with others. See opposite for ideas on how to ensure your child develops his understanding of shared knowledge.

MAKING CONVERSATIONS WORK

Conversations have been compared to delicate plants – if you do not water and feed them in the correct way they die. However, I think it is much better to think of a conversation as being like a game of catch. In a conversation, just as in a game of catch, all the elements have to be present in equal parts to make it work. If any one of these three elements – speaker, message, listener – is missing, the conversation will die.

You might think that the lack of a listener is the most obvious reason for a conversation dying, but this can also happen if the speaker is unaware of her role or if she makes the message too difficult.

We have all spoken to people who don't look at us when we are talking to them and this doesn't feel very comfortable. A listener who doesn't look at the speaker communicates a lack of interest in what is being said, and the lack of feedback makes it difficult for the speaker to judge whether the message has been understood.

The interactive skills that your child developed as a baby will begin to flourish in the toddler years. There are many skills associated with conversations and they all need to be practised over and over again for your child to be able to communicate effectively with adults and peers. As in a game of catch, she has to refine her skills both as a 'sender' and a 'receiver', that is, a speaker and a listener, until she becomes really expert.

Not only will your child have to learn 'how' to talk but she will need to know how to 'give' and 'receive' information effectively. Now you will see the range of skills she needs.

BEING A GOOD LISTENER

Being a good listener is the most important skill to give your child. As a good listener, she will always be watching the speaker and should then acquire the skills necessary to be a good speaker too.

However, there is a huge difference between 'listening skills' and the 'listener's role', and by understanding this you will be able to recognise any difficulties your child is having with the listener's role.

Listening skills are important for language development. They include the child being able to:

- listen to the sound — that is, actually hear it
- tell the difference between sounds, for example 'b' and 's'

- remember a number of sounds or words, for example 'c' + 'a' + 't' = cat
- repeat the same order of the sounds — 'b-a-g' rather than 'gab'.

If your child can do all this, you may conclude or be told that your child has good 'listening skills'. But does she really have the skills associated with being a good listener?

WHAT A LISTENER HAS TO DO
Without the listener looking at her or providing useful feedback, the speaker will find it really hard to continue to give sufficient and relevant information. Consider how people giving talks find it hard to do this straight after lunch, when the feedback from the audience is reduced as they digest their food or quietly nod off!

I often ask children what they think makes a good listener and mostly they tell me 'listening' makes a good listener. If you then ask how we know others are listening, they have no idea. It is important to know that your listener is listening, because only then will you know whether what you are saying makes sense to them. We saw in 'Conversational skills' in Part One, page 24, what a listener needs to do, but for your child who is starting to develop these skills, you need to make sure she can:

1. look at the speaker
2. be still while listening
3. listen — she needs to demonstrate this by talking about the same thing as the speaker.

By focusing on these three basic elements of what a listener has to do, the other necessary skills should develop as a natural consequence.

Looking at the speaker The first of these skills is the most important. As long you have been encouraging facial interest since your child was born you should have no worries about whether or not she looks at the speaker. However, if she still needs prompting to look at people, simply investigate to see if she can process what she sees in people's faces and bodies: are they 'happy', 'upset' or 'worried'? (Look back at 'What does that mean?', page 70.)

Simply telling your child to 'make eye contact' is a waste of time. If she doesn't know the purpose of looking at people, she will not be able to interpret the non-verbal information. Without this skill your daughter will not learn the benefit of looking at people and is likely to stop.

If your child enjoys looking at facial expressions and body language, and has gained from doing so, looking at faces is already meaningful to her. If she doesn't look at faces automatically, you need to go back a stage or two and develop her interest in faces and in understanding of what body language means. Until her interpretational skills are present, it is of no benefit to ask her to look at the person she is talking to.

Don't assume that she is choosing not to look at you or that she is merely diffident; before the age of five, your child **has** to look at people many, many times a day to become a proficient communicator later in her life.

Keeping still The second skill in the list is associated with many communication difficulties and often improves automatically when a child becomes able to process non-verbal information.

If your child keeps still while communicating, she will be able to look at the other person and will be focused on listening to the message. Being fidgety, on the other hand, or moving around too much gets in the way of taking in non-verbal information. Once she is able to understand that the information she picks up is useful to her, **then she will keep still.**

You are less likely to continue to talk to a person who moves about constantly during the conversation. Therefore, children who do this are unlikely to maintain or keep

Not looking at speaker
One of these children is not looking at the teacher and so isn't listening to what she is saying.

WHAT CAN HAPPEN?

I once saw a child who was the son of a health worker. When I assessed him, it became obvious that his father knew that 'eye contact' was important. I observed the child during a 20-minute 'on the mat' session in the classroom. The teacher spoke for the whole 20 minutes and every other child in the class had started to get restless. The child I was going to assess was the only one sitting still and looking at the teacher throughout the session!

At the end of the session, I asked the child what the teacher had been talking about. He said 'I don't know!' and looked at me as if I was mad to ask the question. This young boy had no idea why he was looking at the teacher; he just knew it was what his father wanted him to do.

friendships — simply because the basic building block of friendships is the ability to hold effective conversations. Fidgeting while someone is talking to you communicates a lack of interest or focus, so her friends may go and talk to someone else who is a better listener.

Being able to listen The third skill might appear to be self-evident but, while most of the children I have worked with have some idea that being a 'good listener' is important, they have little idea what it means in practice. I ask children 'How do I know you are listening?' They may say 'You need to look', but generally they are unaware of the need to be still and have no idea that the key evidence that someone is listening is when they respond appropriately. The listener must reply on the same topic.

TRY THIS!

Get someone who doesn't see your child every day, such as Grandad, to do this. 'Prime' him to do the following:

- He must look at your daughter and she must look at him.
- Grandad must also be still throughout!
- Then say to your daughter, 'Ask Grandad what he had for breakfast'.
- If she doesn't know how to ask this, tell her, 'Say "What did you have for breakfast, Grandad?"'
- When your daughter first asks what he had for breakfast, he should answer the question by saying something completely different, like 'It was snowing this morning – wasn't it fun?'
- When Grandad gives the wrong answer, talk to her about whether or not he was listening; point out that he was sitting still and looking, but did he really listen? She should recognise that he did not listen because he didn't answer her question.
- Then get her to ask the question once more and this time Grandad is a good listener because he does all three elements.
- She repeats: 'What did you have for breakfast, Grandad?'
- Tell him that this time, he is to answer correctly, such as 'I had toast and a cup of tea.'

This exercise helps your daughter realise that only when she speaks about the same topic or responds to a question in the expected way will you know that she is really listening. Children who have difficulty with this are often said to be 'not sticking to topic' and it is a clear indication that they don't yet understand how to be a good listener.

... AND THIS!

If your daughter is having difficulty looking at the speaker or sitting still, use this little exercise slightly differently by getting her to tell you something she is really interested in, making sure she looks at you while doing so. As soon as she starts telling you her 'news', turn away or start to fidget. It makes more impact if you do these actions separately, even if she tends to do both at once.

What happens is that fidgeting, or not looking at her, stops her from being able to talk to you and she won't like it! Children who fidget or don't look at you during a conversation usually have little appreciation of the impact of their behaviour. By doing this simple exercise, your child will start to know how it affects the conversation.

Finally, don't do these things just once. Make a game of it and help her every day if possible to realise that these three skills are vital elements when listening to people. Don't forget to exaggerate your tone of voice and body language as you go!

Once your daughter has learned to be a 'good listener' and knows that she needs to look at the person she is communicating with and that she needs to be still, you can then give her a simple reminder if now and then she doesn't look at you or keep still. Just say, 'Are you ready to talk?' I use this prompt with children very early on in the intervention programme and I find they are then able to remember that they must look at me and they automatically make themselves ready to listen.

This is a wonderful technique for helping your child get ready to do anything, as long as she knows the 'rules' for a situation. For instance, when you need her to get her coat and shoes on, say '**Are you ready** to go out?' Or, at school, when she needs to be still and focus for work, her teacher could say '**Are you ready** to work?' or '**Are you ready** to read?' Don't forget that, as with all Not Just Talking strategies, you must repeat these phrases in the same way until she has responded in the way you want.

GIVING FEEDBACK AS A LISTENER
During these toddler years, your child must learn how to give feedback during a conversation. In normal development, children of this age go through a phase of asking for endless feedback verbally. This is often through the use of the word 'Why?' It may sometimes drive you to distraction, but don't stop her, because it is doing two important things:

- It gives your child experience of being able to ask for clarification in a supportive environment at home. (By the time she goes to school, she should have toned down her requests and also be starting to use other non-verbal ways of asking for clarification.)
- She is accumulating knowledge about the world that will be very helpful in terms of both her vocabulary and her ability to process non-verbal clues in day-to-day situations, for example 'Why are you fixing the plug, Mummy?' Children who don't watch their parents, or don't listen to communication about everyday activities around the home, fail to learn the vocabulary associated with these activities.

You need to help your child communicate non-verbally about what she understands and what she is finding confusing, so that when she is listening she is automatically giving clear, non-verbal feedback, telling the speaker whether she:

- is interested in what is being said
- understands the message
- needs more information
- wants different information.

Another important but more demanding conversational skill that evolves at this stage is her ability to demonstrate interest in what other people are saying – a vital part of your child's capacity to make and keep friends. A child who fails to demonstrate interest in what another child says, will find that over time other children become less likely to engage her in a conversation. We all want to know that people are interested in what we have to say – even young children (see box on page 94 for more on sharing information).

This underlines the importance of the basic give-and-take of a conversation and understanding the listener's role in keeping the conversation alive. An uninterested listener can kill a conversation just as easily as someone who talks too much about a subject of little interest to others. If you don't show interest in the game of catch you are likely to drop the ball, and your partner may give up and walk away.

WHAT A SPEAKER NEEDS TO DO
Learning how to speak is not just about learning to talk. Verbal language skills are important, but here I will be talking about the role of the speaker and what a speaker has to do to keep the conversation going and make it successful.

It is the speaker's 'job' to judge the best way to get the message across to the listener. This involves a combination of skills – prediction, turn-taking, language skills, and so on. Here you will see the skills your child needs to learn in order to become a good speaker. These include:

1. Thinking about what – if anything – the listener already knows about what the topic. This is based on her understanding of the information that her listener already has.

2. Adjusting the message according to how much or how little the listener knows already.

3. Making sure the words she chooses are meaningful to her listener.

4. Making sure her style is suitable for her listener and the situation; for example using different ways to talk to friends, parents, teachers or strangers.

5. Making sure that what she says is appropriate. For example, in some situations she can talk about personal matters, in others she shouldn't. (Can you think of situations like this? What clues tell you this?)

6. Looking at her listener.

7. Being able to interpret non-verbal feedback and making sure that her listener receives the message as she intended.

8. Checking out her listener's understanding of the message.

9. Repeating, changing or elaborating the message if necessary.

As you can see, there are many skills that your child must develop simply to be good at giving information to others!

WHAT CAN HAPPEN?

The Stuart family have read several books that tell them to talk to their child. They thought she was listening to them and watching, and that she would develop conversational skills on her own. Now she is four, they say that she is shy and doesn't like talking to strangers, even though the strangers are not strangers because they have been introduced into the conversation by her parents. Since she first became 'shy', she has started rushing off at the prospect of meeting different people. The Stuarts thought that she would be fine when she started school the next year, but she really struggled.

The Williams family read *Not Just Talking* when their little girl was a baby. They realised that, unless they make an effort and gave her opportunities every day to practise talking and listening to different people in different situations, she wouldn't have the skills to benefit from conversations when she gets to school.

So they set up situations where she can practise talking to shop assistants, school-crossing attendants, the doctor, health visitor or her parents' friends. Now they are pleased because she is four and most of the time is giving good information of the right type and quantity to people other than her family.

Let's look at this book
This mum and her child are sharing this book. The girl is looking at her mum while she talks about what she sees in the book. The mum can make sure her child has understood by asking her about the pictures they can both see.

LET'S START AT THE BEGINNING

The ability to give messages is often one that is overlooked as many professionals put the focus on children's ability to understand what is being said – that is, the language. Language is important, of course, but if your child cannot also spontaneously send messages to others, she will be disadvantaged throughout her life.

I have seen many children who are able to give only limited messages and so are restricted in new situations. This leads to frustration and anxiety. Two children I have seen in the last 16 years were

CASE HISTORY

Here is an example of a child unable to give messages by any means. He is still mostly non-verbal but is now using a handheld computer and communicating exceptionally well.

Brian was seven, in mainstream education, and in his pre-school years he had a tremendous amount of support from Portage, applied behaviour analysis (ABA), speech and language therapy, as well as other interventions.

When I first saw him, I was told he was 'just about to speak' as he was able to say a 'b' sound. Because everything else sounded very positive, I thought my help would not be needed. There were no behaviour issues and he was not a problem in school. However, his mother was very keen for me to see him, so I agreed to assess him.

When I arrived in his Year 2 classroom, Brian was sitting at a table immediately in front of the teacher, with one or two other children. There was a learning support assistant sitting next to Brian. I observed what was happening for a few minutes. The class teacher told the assistant what she wanted Brian to do, and the assistant told Brian. He did the activity, then he stopped. The assistant noticed that he had stopped and told the teacher, who then gave some more work to the assistant for Brian.

I was astounded that there was no frustration in him: he couldn't respond or send messages apart from a very few basic things. Those supporting him had not noticed this. Within two weeks of my involvement, he was taught to sign and had learned so many signs that very soon he was combining them into sentences.

My view is that every child needs to be able to communicate and that speech is not the only way to achieve this. Also, if the child's non-verbal skills lag a long way behind their age level, you need to focus on developing these skills before thinking that the child will talk. Because most people had expected Brian to talk, he missed out on five or six years when he could have been learning more appropriate communication skills.

After the excitement about his sudden ability to ask for what he wanted, I asked myself 'Why isn't he talking?' I was horrified to discover that he had one of the severest examples of articulatory dyspraxia (see 'What does that mean?', opposite) that I had ever seen. On assessment at seven, despite having the biggest appetite for food and absolutely no problem at all chewing and swallowing, Brian was totally unable to open his mouth when asked to do so.

Brian could use signing to communicate instead of speech, which he was a long way from achieving. Within two weeks of signing, he developed language skills and over the next few months began to give his mother so many complex messages she could hardly keep up!

WHAT DOES THAT MEAN?

Articulatory dyspraxia is a condition where words can be spoken and sounds made spontaneously but not when you try to do so. It is easier to understand in adults who have been able to talk well all their life and then, as a result of a stroke or some other head injury, they become 'dyspraxic' with regard to articulation of words for speech.

For these adults, it means that if you said 'Would you like a cup of ...', they could add 'tea' because it is an automatic response that they don't even have to think about. However, if you said 'What are you drinking?' they would struggle and be unable to say the word 'tea'. People with articulatory dyspraxia are sometimes able to sing or repeat poems learned as a child without difficulty.

If you apply this to children, however, it is very different. As we saw earlier, because children have no memory of how to make the sounds, it causes them difficulty. Not only will they struggle to make the sound consistently, but they will also have great difficulty in sequencing sounds. The particular boy in the case history opposite, Brian, was so severely affected that he couldn't even make a speech sound that was of use to him and he certainly couldn't sequence sounds for words.

If your child has a difficulty with making sounds consistently or sequencing sounds, please seek the advice of a speech and language therapist as soon as possible.

totally unable to give messages — a really worrying situation to be in. Encourage your child to give, as well as receive, messages.

HELP HER TO BECOME A GOOD SPEAKER

Your child's ability to send messages — to tell you something, to express a need, to comment — starts before she acquires language or begins to talk. This is why I recommended in Part One (page 34) that you teach your baby signs from an early age (before she can sign herself) and encourage her to ask for items of food or toys or activities. If you have followed this advice, she will naturally start to send messages when she begins communicating through spoken language.

NAMING OBJECTS, ACTIONS AND PEOPLE

When language starts, it begins at a single-word level of communication. All children start here: they do not start by talking in sentences. Only when she has a variety of single words will your child be able to put words together to form sentences. However, without the skill to name objects, actions and people, she will find using the language in more sophisticated ways very difficult.

To encourage your daughter's ability to do this, keep most of what you say to her at the level of her language development. So, when she is able to say one word, the majority of comments you make to her should be in the form of single words. For example, when you see an object that you know she doesn't have the word for, just name it. Say simply 'elephant'; don't try to make it sound better by adding other words — 'Look at the lovely elephant', for instance. Instead, add other non-verbal clues, such as pretending your arm is the trunk and making an elephant-like noise. These additional, non-verbal signals help your little girl learn the new word more easily through association with a total of three prompts, rather than simply the spoken word.

She should also start to identify what she sees: 'cat', 'dinner', 'Daddy' and so on. This step doesn't happen by magic but only after observing cats frequently enough to identify the features that are common to them. This must be combined with the experience of hearing the word 'cat' whenever she sees one — the more often the better.

Part of this process will include pointing at the cat, or even picking the cat up and letting your child stroke it. The focus of the 'conversation' will be the cat, even if it's just in a photograph (which of course will also be developing the ability to understand symbolisation; see 'Related skills', page 121).

Your child will also have learned through observation that people's eyes go towards the target object or event being spoken about, but only if she has developed interest in watching people. As a result, she too will look at what is being talked about as this is modelled to her. A common problem is that children often do not look at what is being spoken about and therefore they cannot store and use the experience in a manner that is useful to them in other situations. This means they can't 'generalise'. (For more on this, see pages 80, 130.)

Even if your child is a teenager but is still communicating only at a one-word level, remember that when you talk to her you must keep your spoken language at the level at which she is communicating.

HAS SHE STARTED TO PUT WORDS TOGETHER?
When your child has developed a range of single words and is moving towards putting them together, you need to 'model' two-word utterances to her. Modelling (in this context) is simlply the process

WHAT CAN HAPPEN?

I sometimes encounter children of between seven and 15, or even older, who others think are communicating very well through language. These children learn to speak purely through copying what others say and can sometimes repeat whole sentences or 'stories' in apparently the right situation. For example, when asked what they enjoy doing at school, they might say something like 'School is nice, we do golden time'. This sounds like a suitable response but isn't in fact answering the question, and if you ask another similar question, such as 'What happens in the playground at school?', you might well get the same reply. The thing that stimulates the production of the sentence may simply be the word 'school'.

The child appears to be able to talk in long and grammatically correct sentences. However, through the Not Just Talking assessment, it becomes clear that when asked a variety of specific questions, she can give only single-word responses. This can come as a shock to both parents and school staff, who see the child as a 'good' communicator.

Similarities and differences
Here are three very different cats and two dogs, one of which looks similar to a cat. Interpretation is quite difficult because it is mainly our past experience that tells us the second animal from the right is a dog. All three cats are similar in colour but very different in markings.

of you talking in a manner that you wish your child to use later in situations on her own. (For other aspects of modelling, see 'Making sense of it all', pages 44, 70)

If you repeat only one word, your child is more likely to continue using one word at a time and her language skills won't develop. You don't want her to copy everything you say; if she does this, she will only learn to repeat words parrot-fashion. If she copies you for a short time, she should soon be using and initiating two-word utterances that are relevant to what she sees.

If you talk in longer sentences, your little girl may not learn how to build them up for herself. The modelling of two-word utterances by adults or siblings also develops your child's use of new types of language, for example verbs, adjectives, adverbs, possessive nouns. Most of the time you will do this instinctively, but frequent repetition is helpful. The development of language is a cumulative stage-by-stage process; if you try to fast-forward it, she will not be able to use language meaningfully.

DEVELOPING MEANING

When your child is able to put two words together easily, you need to think about adding in the words that make it sound more like natural speech. You can also extend the number of words your child can string together, so that she will be able to talk in two- and three-word phrases. This is achieved by adding to the first thing that she says, for example 'cat'. You could extend this by saying something like 'Yes, it's a black cat' or 'It's a fat cat'. This is often called 'extending the utterance'.

Basically, you are helping your little girl in exactly the same way as before ('modelling' what you want her to say), but you are increasing the number of words and the complexity of the sentence structure step by step.

The use of phrases such as 'All gone!' can develop into 'Car gone' or 'Granny gone'. The words 'Bye bye' are useful at this stage as long as they have been encouraged before the baby starts to talk. Modelling 'Bye bye Daddy', 'Bye

bye postman', 'Bye bye bricks' or 'Bye bye plane' helps the child understand not only the two-word utterances but also the situations associated with particular words. It can also be a stepping stone to producing two-word utterances — she might use the gesture and 'Wave', then add the word 'Daddy'.

These words can also continue to develop your child's recognition that something is finishing. She should notice — as long as she is looking — when you wave at whoever is leaving and will associate the body language and the common circumstance of 'going away'.

After many occasions when two-word utterances are modelled to your child, she will start to put words together, for example 'Daddy gone' or 'Nappy now'. These two-word utterances lead to her being able to use language in different ways, such as requesting information or asking for

TRY THIS!

- Help her by encouraging two words instead of one.
- When she says just one word, such as 'giraffe', say to her 'Yes, look giraffe' or 'Yes, tall giraffe' or 'Yes, hungry giraffe.'
- Mix it up: sometimes repeat just one word she says and sometimes expand it to two words.
- Make it fun!
- 'Nana' can become 'Mashed banana' or 'Yellow banana' or 'Chopped banana'. Accept how she pronounces the words. All you need to do is repeat them in the adult manner. So, if she says 'Nana', you say 'Yes, banana'.
- 'Bike' can become 'Daddy's bike' or 'Red bike' or 'Fast bike' or 'Broken bike' or 'Wet bike'.

Let your imagination go, but keep it related to what you see.

a change of activity, for example. This is an essential feature of being able to give useful information spontaneously to others.

When she has a wide vocabulary and is putting words together, you can start to communicate in longer phrases and sentences. However, your aim at this time should also be to build up her vocabulary. Hiding new words in a long phrase or sentence may make it harder for her to learn and retain them.

WHAT DOES THAT MEAN?

Nouns, verbs, adjectives, adverbs, possessive nouns

Most of us tend to think we have little idea about grammar, but we know more than we think because subconsciously (just as we use our non-verbal understanding) we are using grammar all the time to communicate meaningful sentences.

Here is a simple explanation of key aspects of grammar that you can help her with (the different parts of speech are italicised):

1. Noun – this is the name of an object or activity or person: '*boat*', '*cricket*', '*Joanna*'.

2. Verbs – these are the 'doing' words in a sentence that tell us what the person or object is doing: the boy *kicks* the ball, Mummy *reads*, or my teacher *is* cross.

3. Adjectives – these are the 'describing' words that you can add to a noun: '*red* boat', '*long* boat', '*plain* boat', '*angry* man', '*clever* girl'.

4. Adverbs – these are 'describing' words for verbs. They tell us how and when things happen: 'riding *cautiously*', 'walking *quickly*', 'eating *noisily*', 'talk *tomorrow*', or 'singing *cheerfully*'. As you can easily see, they are mostly formed by adding 'ly' to the adjective, so 'cheerful' the adjective becomes 'cheerfully' the adverb.

5. Possessive nouns – these simply relate to words that describe belonging and are made by adding an apostrophe before or after 's' to a word: '*Mummy's* bag', 'the *cat's* tail' or, when talking about more than one thing or person, 'the *boats'* red sails'.

6. Pronouns – stand for nouns.
  • Personal pronouns are words like '*I*' or '*me*', '*we*' or '*us*', '*they*' or '*them*', '*you*'.
  • Pronouns are the everyday words that we use to stop us from having to repeat the same word over and over. Instead of saying 'We are looking for Mummy's bag. Have you seen Mummy's bag?' you can say 'We are looking for Mummy's bag. Have you seen *it*?' By using the pronoun 'it' you don't have to repeat 'Mummy's bag'.
  • Possessive pronouns are therefore words such as '*mine*', '*his*', '*her*', '*their*' or '*hers*', '*theirs*'.
  • Pronouns also are words like '*who*?' '*which*?' '*this*' and '*that*', and the less specific ones like '*another*', '*all*', '*none*', '*everybody*' – because all these words stand for other information.

You don't need to know the names of these elements of language, but do remember how useful they are for your child communicatively as she wants to expand what she is saying.

THE SOUND OF HER VOICE

Alongside her verbal skill development, you must not forget the intonation, stress and rhythm of her speech. This includes making sure her intonation pattern is pleasant to listen to. Children who speak on one tone — ie, in a 'monotonous' voice — are often less interesting to listen to and sometimes hard to understand as a result.

Rhythm means that her speech should sound like this — la di dah di dah di dah — which is the English language rhythm pattern used in the UK and USA. However, in other countries such as South Africa (which has developed English through Afrikaans), the way they speak English has a different rhythm. They use what is called a 'ratatat' or syllable-timed pattern. Taken to an extreme this ratatat pattern, along with poor use of stress, can sound 'Dalek-like' and would make your child really stand out from her friends.

If you think your child is having difficulty with this aspect of her communication development, you should pay great attention to repeating nursery rhymes with her at least once a day. The poems of children's writers such as AA Milne, Dr Seuss, Alan Ahlberg and Michael Rosen are also full of these rhythms and intonation patterns. The more you read poems to and with your child, the more she will get the rhythm into her brain and the more likely she will be to use it for herself.

TAKING TURNS

One of the most annoying problems facing parents is the inability of some children to take turns. They butt in, fail to give way and may dominate the conversation totally. Your child needs to be able to take turns in a conversation, keep to the topic and give way to her listener from time to time. In the past it was thought that playing turn-taking board games would help a child develop these skills, but communication skills are more subtle than waiting your turn in a game.

Mum reading to two girls
These two girls are listening carefully to poems and are talking about them. They will be picking up and practising intonation skills.

Encourage your child's understanding of turn-taking by doing or saying something, stopping, leaving an obvious gap and waiting for her to make a response. Help her recognise what tells you when it is your turn (see below and 'Try this!', opposite).

Once her skills are starting to grow, your child will also need to notice when to interrupt and when not to do so. Draw her attention to the times when you interrupt each other at home by saying, before you do it, 'I am going to interrupt Mummy', then interrupt and afterwards reflect on why it was OK to do this. Also point out to your child the occasions on which she interrupts in an appropriate way. Praise her by saying something like 'Good turn-taking' to let her know this is what you want her to do in future or explain clearly why she shouldn't do this if it is inappropriate.

As your child grows older, her skills continue to develop so that she is able to take her turn in conversations confidently and at the appropriate point, without the need for you to draw her attention to the pointers any more.

My ten-month-old grandson has developed such good non-verbal conversational skills, he will watch someone talk and then look to the listener knowing that they are going to respond. I am sure he is picking up the signals!

HOW DO YOU KNOW WHEN IT'S YOUR TURN TO TALK?

To do this you need to see a variety of non-verbal clues:

1. There is a pause.

2. The speaker looks at you.

3. You recognise from the intonation pattern that the speaker is about to finish what they are saying and that there will be a pause where you can take your turn.

4. The speaker points at you.

5. You are introduced to the group by the speaker and they turn towards you.

6. The speaker makes a facial expression that says 'Over to you'.

7. The speaker taps his foot and looks at you as if tired of waiting for you to speak.

8. There is a questioning intonation pattern – 'Hungry?'

9. The speaker asks a direct question – 'Where are you going?'

10. Another verbal clue would come from the predicted order of words and their grammatical function, the vocabulary, syntax or grammar. For example, if you heard someone saying 'Would you …', you are likely to know that the person is asking a question. Using contextual clues, you might even predict what follows, perhaps: '… like to go swimming?' This would prepare you to give an answer. However, if you didn't pick this up because you didn't know the important words to listen to and your understanding of grammatical structures was not sufficiently developed, then you would have to wait until the end of the utterance and have less time to get your answer ready. Prediction, as you can see, is not only a huge skill with regard to non-verbal communication but also vital for our language skills.

11. Another spoken clue is that you can predict a question from the words used and their order, for example 'Are you ready?' or 'Is it time for tea?'

SHARING INFORMATION

This means being able to ask others about things that interest them and then being able to make relevant comments or relate what they say to your own similar experiences. This skill is very different from 'Shared knowledge', which I described earlier in 'Who am I?' (see page 93). The ability to 'share information' starts to develop

TRY THIS!

Play lots of give-and-take games, which promote your child's ability to wait their turn and pay attention to what is being done by the other person. To make full use of these types of games, help her to focus on the signs that tell her when it is her turn, or someone else's, to talk.

Many games you play with your child can be adjusted very simply to give her a chance to ask you for information. Otherwise it is easy to fall into a habit of anticipating what she wants. Simple posting games can offer her the chance to ask you for the next object to post. To achieve this, you 'guard' the objects and give her one only when she makes a request for it. There is nothing mean about this, and remember it is beneficial to her communication development.

Think of activities or games that you play with her and work out how to adjust the situation so that she needs to ask you for objects or information. When she is able to talk, games like 'Happy Families' are good as she will be able to practise her asking skill over and over again.

The best game to play at this time is 'Guess Who?' by Hasbro. It will give you many opportunities to make sure she can take turns. It also requires a relatively high level of spoken language understanding so you will be promoting her language skills as well! But she will enjoy playing it with you and will learn

many conversational skills in the process. She will also need to understand the word 'secret' to play this game. If she can't, then play as her partner and have another person play against you, to 'model' how to keep something secret.

Use the following rules to promote good turn-taking and other conversational skills:

1. Is she looking at you when asking the questions?

2. Help her ask questions such as 'Is yours a woman?' She needs to ask questions that can be answered either 'yes' or 'no'.

3. Then, when you have answered, confirm with her which people she is going to turn over. For example, if you say 'No, mine is not a woman', then help your child understand that this means that she turns over all the women. As soon as she has finished turning the pictures over, get her to look at you to let you know that she has finished. Also get her to say 'It's your turn'.

4. Then you can ask her your question.

5. When she answers, confirm with her what you will do as a result, as in **3.** above. Look at her when asking your question and also when you have finished turning over the cards on your tray to let her know it is now her turn and help her to see the importance of doing this.

when your child is about four and has good all-round communication.

During this phase of her life, your child needs to realise that conversations are not simply one-way traffic — an important progression from learning just to give or receive. Children who are only able to 'talk' and can't share find it difficult to maintain the interest of others. Sharing what you know with others is the basic tool of friendship and the secret of good conversations.

Your child needs to be able to show interest in others by asking questions. You can model this to him by asking about some of these topics:

- how they are and what they have been doing
- family and friends, who may have common experiences and interests — he will learn what worked for them and what didn't
- the topic they are talking about
- what is happening in the situation they are in
- what they like to do — toys she likes to play with, or games or activities such as face painting or ballet or riding a bike
- what music they like listening to
- TV programmes or films that they like
- what sport they like to play or watch.

WHAT CAN YOU DO?
To make this 'sharing' even more successful, your child needs to learn to be aware of the feedback from her listener and adjust what she is saying to meet her listener's needs.

Help your child to ask questions about what you and others are doing, what you like or don't like and so on. Do this by asking your child what she thought about something she has done: 'Did you like going to the park with Grandad?' Then say to Grandad, 'Was it good going to the park with Daisy' and 'I like going to the park with Daisy too.'

By giving good examples like this in many different situations, your child should start to learn about the benefit of sharing information. Another approach is to ask 'What did you do at playgroup?' When she has told you, prompt her to ask you the same type of question: say 'Ask me what I did while you were at playgroup.' Also get

her to ask her brothers and sisters what they have been doing or what Mummy did at work.

Talk about situations in books where it is obvious that characters are sharing information about what they are doing or might be going to do. The Oxford Reading Tree books are very good for this (for more about using this set of books, see 'Troublesome children', page 138). It will also be helpful to make suggestions about what others might do or what your child should do in particular situations.

CAN SHE TALK IN GROUP SITUATIONS?
During this period of being a toddler and developing all these essential conversational skills, your child will go from being able to talk to one person at a time — you, her sibling or her carer — to being able to talk in small groups and, eventually, larger groups. This development is a necessary step to take before school. Without the ability to cope with groups, your child will find life at school overpowering.

So what is the difference between speaking in a one-to-one situation and in a small group? In a one-to-one situation you have only one person's body language and facial expressions to read and, therefore, just need to adjust what you say to one person's requirements. In any situation where there is more than one person, the need to be aware of non-verbal feedback increases for each person added to the group. This is why large groups are so much more challenging to our conversational skills; even some adults avoid these!

Try to give your child opportunities to talk and listen to more than one person at a time. Help her look for the clues that tell you when it is your turn to talk or how to identify the topic of conversation or how to adjust what you are saying to multiple listeners. Talk about how you know all these things.

CAN SHE NEGOTIATE?
Your child needs to learn how to negotiate her way out of conflict. Once again, she will do this by watching how you negotiate in commonplace situations at home. Show your child a range of emotional situations so that she can learn in the security of home how she should deal with these

challenges. The more practice she has, the easier she will find it to develop negotiation skills when interacting with her own age group at school.

Show your little girl how you change your communication to calm situations down and find a point of agreement, for example deciding who is going to take the dog for a walk, or which channel to watch on the TV, or whose turn it is to put the dustbin out!

Just check that your child is watching these conversations, even if they develop into conflict. The more opportunities she has, the easier she will find it to practise these skills when playing with her friends as a toddler and as she begins to take part in playground games. You could also use toy animals or dolls to role play how to deal with conflict and negotiate. The more ways that you can give your child to practise in a safe and non-threatening manner the better.

FOCUS POINTS

★ Think of a conversation as a game of catch – all three elements have to be present for it to work.

★ Help your child look, be still and listen to the person talking to her.

★ Help her learn what information she can get from both the speaker and the listener.

★ Don't tell her 'give me eye contact', simply say 'Look at me.'

★ Help her recognise signs telling her what to do in a situation.

★ Model how to give feedback as a listener and show interest in conversations.

★ Make clear signs that tell her that it's her turn to talk.

★ Use visual or auditory signals about waiting for her turn. If your child doesn't know whose turn it is to talk, you could say 'When I have finished talking to … I will talk to you', ring a bell or use something as a 'talking stick' (the speaker holds this until they have finished talking and then passes it on to the next person who is going to say something; it could be a stick or a stuffed toy which is used for that purpose and nothing else).

★ If you say 'I will talk to you later' make sure you do, otherwise you may find she will not believe you the next time you say it and may behave inappropriately as a result.

★ Organise different situations and experiences with friends, family and people you don't see so often or know so well, so that your child can have the opportunity to develop and practise her skills in a wide range of situations.

★ Get the whole family involved by modelling for her how to expand her grammar as well as helping her try different ways to use language, such as adding adjectives and adverbs.

★ Encourage good intonation, rhythm and stress by doing nursery rhymes and poems every day with her.

★ Encourage giving and sharing information in a variety of situations.

★ Can she talk and listen when she is in a small group – with both peers and adults?

★ Model how you negotiate your way out of family arguments and role-play situations where she can practise simple negotiations.

WHAT TO TALK ABOUT

This chapter focuses on helping your child to request and give information, direct the attention of others to what he can see, ask questions and so on. If he can only operate in one mode, his ability to participate in any kind of conversation will be impeded. Your child's conversational skills need to expand so that he is able to ask for and give information in a wide variety of circumstances.

CAN HE REQUEST INFORMATION?

This is making any overture that seeks a response from the listener. It could be a question or a statement, and might be:

- a personal inquiry – 'How are you?'
- a straightforward question – 'What time is it?'
- seeking an opinion – 'What do you think of the jam tarts?'
- an invitation – 'Would you like to go to the museum?'

- making a statement that prompts a response – 'Your cake is delicious'
- a request for help – 'Can you help me do my shoe lace up?'
- a request for clarification – 'I don't understand what you mean.'

All of these are techniques for starting or maintaining a conversation. Being capable of requesting information in a variety of ways is a key skill in keeping a conversation flowing.

Your child needs to realise that he can actually start a whole conversation himself simply by asking for or giving new details. Non-verbal methods of requesting objects and actions should now develop into spoken requests of increasing length and complexity. Conversation can be initiated in a variety of ways, for example by choosing a game

Fun in the park
These four children are chatting together, but at this point they are listening to the girl at the back of the group as the children at the front are turned towards her.

and bringing it to you to play, offering his sister a piece of his banana or asking you what is going to be happening next.

Many children who fail to develop the skill of initiating conversation can be misdiagnosed as 'attention seeking'. If your child goes up to an adult and looks like he is trying to make contact but then doesn't say anything, you should ask yourself if he is able to initiate conversations in any other situations. He may have learned how to make contact but is unable to take it further and begin a conversation.

Once a conversation is under way, different styles of requesting can be used to explore a topic in more depth, engage someone's interest further and develop the relationship. In any conversation you are by turns requesting and giving information. The latter includes answering a direct question, giving an opinion, offering clarification, or making a statement in response to what has been said to you.

Being able to join in a conversation is a skill that is easily neglected because your child may look like he understands what you are saying but just doesn't respond. Remember that he may not have sufficient non-verbal skills to understand what kind of response is required, and therefore this lack of response is not a deliberate choice on his part.

As we have already seen, your child can only learn to give the necessary information if you don't anticipate his needs. Even if you think you know what he wants for supper, offer him choices (see 'Related skills', page 126 for more on choosing), or wait for him to ask for a book to be passed rather than just giving it to him.

Give him the chance to ask you for the book. If he makes the request non-verbally, either by holding out his hand or by pointing to the book, act on it. If you don't respond to his attempts to communicate, he won't be encouraged to make further requests. Making gestures to get objects is a good step on the way to verbal communication but by now he needs to practise asking questions and making comments on what is happening as well.

Asking him what he wants might feel unnatural, but communication is no different from any other skill: the way to help a child learn to ride a bike is

HOW CAN YOU HELP?

It is sometimes too easy to get a drink for your little boy without giving him the chance to ask for it. You, as a competent communicator with excellent interpretation skills, can respond to all the non-verbal clues. For example:

- He is walking towards the cupboard where the drinking cups are kept.
- It is the time he usually has a drink.
- He looks at the fridge.
- The look on his face tells you he wants a drink.
- He tries to open the fridge door.

Giving him his drink before he asks because you know what he wants doesn't help him practise conveying a message. Give him a chance to practise requesting for himself by asking what he wants.

not to do it for him but to give him a chance to try it out. Likewise, if your child is not given the option to ask for objects and activities, he will not learn to get conversations going.

Prompt him to request something. For example, if your child looks sleepy, you may be thinking he wants to go to bed. To encourage him to communicate what he wants, look at the child and ask him non-verbally what he wants to do — shrug your shoulders and hold out your hands, add

SIGN FOR 'WHAT?'

Closed hand with index finger pointing up waggles from side to side.

a questioning sound 'Huh?' If he doesn't respond, ask him 'What do you want?' Don't take him to his bed unless he has communicated in some way — however small — that this is what he wants to do. This might only be a brief look at the stairs or a sign for 'sleep' but in the period before he can talk, accept this. You want him to say in words what he wants, but if he is not yet able to do so, you must value the communication that he does make. This will encourage him to go on and develop his ability.

Another stage is to offer more advanced choices: 'Do you want to sleep or go for a walk? Choose.' If you don't value your child's attempts at communication, not only will this discourage him but he may become frustrated and resort to other methods — such as tantrums.

MAKING A REPLY
To develop his ability to reply, ask him questions such as 'Where's teddy?' or 'Who ate the biscuit?' or 'What's Daddy done?' If your child is still not talking, he can answer using gesture. So he might point at teddy or at himself in answer to 'Who ate the biscuit?' or he might use words and say 'broken' in response to a plate being dropped.

The most important thing is that you create a variety of different situations in which your child can respond to simple conversational phrases. Remember not to predict what he is thinking or what he wants as this will not help him practise his information-giving skills.

THE USE OF 'PLEASE'
We saw in Part Two (page 63) that if the word 'please' is introduced too early before your child has learned to use a range of nouns or verbs, then 'please' becomes a 'magic word' that does away with the need to learn more vocabulary. If you say 'please' and look at or point to something the likelihood is that you will be given it.

'Please' and 'thank you' are both words that children learn by rote from about the age of two or three, when they have a growing vocabulary, but real understanding of what 'please' and 'thank you' mean is only associated with these words at a later stage — possibly as late as four or five.

WHAT MIGHT HAPPEN?

This problem with learning words simply by copying them also applies to the word 'sorry'. If he learns to say this before his non-verbal processing skills are good enough, he won't learn which behaviour he is apologising for, just that you want him to say the word 'sorry'.

In my experience, parents are often surprised by teenagers who go into rages very easily, go up to their bedrooms and then come down, calmer and say 'sorry', which sounds meaningful to the parents and yet the child repeats the undesired behaviour at a later date. He has learned that his parents want to hear him say 'sorry' and that seems to make them happy, so he says 'sorry' whenever any situation occurs in which he is out of favour with them.

The connection has not been made between the specific behaviour of which his parents disapprove and for which they require an apology. He has simply learned on a 'stimulus-response' basis that when he comes downstairs having been sent to his room, the first word he must say is 'sorry'.

Try to ensure that your child is not repeating words without meaning by not asking him to produce words out of context, for instance 'Say doggie, Peter' when there is no dog present. I appreciate that parents are proud of their child especially when the vocabulary suddenly starts to increase, but you will hear more new words from your child if you keep the talking to what is actually going on.

If his vocabulary is good, then learning these words parrot-fashion is not detrimental, but if he only knows two or three words it will seriously disadvantage his ability to learn more words.

It is better to be certain that he can communicate appropriately in all situations before insisting on the use of 'please' and 'thank you'. These words are merely social conventions and although they are of value in everyday exchanges, they are not fundamental to the message.

ASKING FOR HELP

It is very important to make sure that your child can ask for help from an early age. As adults we do this naturally in the course of a conversation when we don't quite understand what is being said to us. So, if you look confused, the speaker will change what they are saying to help you understand. It is the speaker's job to deliver the message in a suitable manner for their listener.

In everyday conversations we frequently ask for help. This usually happens non-verbally — a raised eyebrow, a shrug of the shoulders, an interrogative intonation pattern, a grunt, and so on. As adults our communication improves when we help each other to understand the message.

If you have been using signing from an early age then 'help' is one of the useful words that your child will have learned. When it looks like he is struggling with something, say 'Do you need help?' Use the sign as well. Then encourage him to ask for 'help' either by signing or saying the word or using both.

Now give your child a chance to develop this skill by encouraging him to ask for help to get drinks or do his shoes up or choose what to wear. By using non-verbal and verbal cues you can make certain this skill develops so that, as he becomes more proficient in conversations, he will ask for help himself when he needs it.

If you can do this at least every day for even just a few weeks then he will learn to do it himself

spontaneously. Soon he will be asking for help through words and then later through facial expressions and body language too! Being able to ask for help, especially when he gets to school, not only enables him to make sense of what is going on around him but improves his ability to learn, deepens his understanding and expands his store of experience.

LANGUAGE STYLES

Language styles are the different types of conversation that we all have every day. Think of all the different people you will talk to each day and reflect on the various styles in which you communicate, from intimate to casual to formal and so on.

It is important that your child notices this difference in the way you communicate with different people and sees what it is that makes you adopt different styles. I often come across children who talk in exactly the same manner to everyone. This can be monotonous and dominating as well as inappropriate; for instance, they may talk to the head teacher using the playground silliness they might enjoy with their friends.

Talk to your toddler about this aspect of your communication, drawing attention to it in a light-hearted way, for example 'Did you see how seriously Mummy talked to that policeman?', and talk to your child about the style you used and why you might change style.

Asking for help
This girl has asked her mum to help her get her top off because she is stuck. It's important that children know how to ask for help.

Often the style of conversation we apply is based on what people wear — think about vicars, doctors, nurses, shop assistants, farmers, plumbers, etc. Also talk about using informal styles with family and friends and formal styles with teachers, doctors, nurses, and so on.

Watch your child to see if he realises that talking to his friend's parents needs a different style from when he is talking to the school crossing attendant outside his siblings' school. (Really this should have happened by the time he is four years old, in preparation for entry to school).

An older child in school who has not learned to recognise this aspect of non-verbal communication will talk to teachers, peers and visitors to the school in exactly the same manner. This usually doesn't go down well!

TRY THIS!

Two Fat Gentlemen
Another good way to promote different styles of talking is through nursery rhymes. 'Two fat gentlemen' is a really good one as it has so many different people who are saying the same thing in different ways. For each of these verses change the voice, speed and volume of saying 'How do you do?' according to the character:

1. Two fat gentlemen met in the lane,
Bowed most politely, bowed once again.
How do you do? How do you do?
How do you do again?

2. Two thin ladies met in the lane,
Bowed most politely, bowed once again.
How do you do? How do you do?
How do you do again?

3. Two tall policemen met in the lane,
Bowed most politely, bowed once again.
How do you do? How do you do?
How do you do again?

4. Two little schoolboys met in a lane,
Bowed most politely, bowed once again.
How do you do? How do you do?
How do you do again?

5. Two little babies met in a lane,
Bowed most politely, bowed once again.
How do you do? How do you do?
How do you do again?

FOCUS POINTS

★ Don't anticipate what your child wants – give him a chance to practise asking you for it.

★ Ask him questions – wait for a response, verbal or non-verbal – then act on it.

★ Don't insist on the use of 'please' or 'sorry' until you are certain his non-verbal interpretation is developed sufficiently for him to understand the significance of these words.

★ Encourage him to ask for help.

★ Talk about the different ways people communicate depending on the situation.

★ Help him recognise the similarities and differences in the ways people hold conversations.

★ Nursery rhymes are good for learning different styles of conversations.

★ Don't forget that eating round a table is the ideal opportunity to practise all these skills.

MAKING AND KEEPING FRIENDS

Early experience of making friends helps your child become a confident and contented adult. Any child who lacks conversational skills will be disadvantaged when it comes to building friendships. She will need to talk about things that interest her peers. Just giving information is not enough; your child needs to be able to listen to what is said to her so she can reply in a way that is useful and/or interesting to her friends. Friendships grow through sharing information about activities, interests and feelings. This is all achieved through conversation. Much is learned while falling in and out of friendships.

STARTING FRIENDSHIPS
The first chance your toddler has to make friends may be when she starts at playgroup or nursery. But some children are only used to playing on their own. When she first arrives at playgroup, your child needs to be aware of other children so that she can join in and share things.

By doing things together, listening to a story, playing or eating, conversations occur and she will find she has things in common with other children. There has to be a topic of shared interest for communication to happen, but your child soon finds out that others laugh at the same jokes, enjoy the same activities or have similar family circumstances, and from these early beginnings friendships will develop.

The biggest challenge will be when she enters school. She has to quickly make new friends through talking about what is happening, rather than just what is important to her. She also needs to take an interest in the other children in her class.

What are little boys made of?
These boys are about the same age so are friends rather than brothers. Another clue is that they look very different: one has curly hair and the other very straight hair.

HOW TO HELP YOUR CHILD MAKE FRIENDS

To give your child the best chance of learning to make friends, arrange for other children to come to play at your house. Organise something for the children to do. Left to her own devices, your child may not know how to start up conversations.

At first you will need to demonstrate to your child how to make friends through modelling a conversation. Show this by asking your child's friend questions such as how many brothers and sisters they have, what's their favourite toy, what games they like to play.

Also demonstrate how interested you are in what they say and ask supplementary questions about what the child tells you. If you are told, for example, that the child went to the park with her Mum, ask her what things she likes to do at the park. If she says she likes the ice-creams, then ask what flavour she likes and then tell the child what flavour you like or your child likes. Ask your child

to give the answers to some of these types of questions too.

What you are doing is showing your child how a conversation flows back and forth. Remember how important modelling adult behaviour is for developing skills in your child. Some children will need a lot more experience than others, so don't give up. Offering her a choice, at the start and during an activity, is another way to help your child practise sharing information. She will be able to talk about what she has chosen and why. Encourage your child to ask her friend to choose as well.

THE DIFFERENCE BETWEEN MAKING AND KEEPING FRIENDS

To make friends your child might go up to another child and say 'Hello, my name is . . .' and then tell them what she is interested in or ask them to join in a game. Quite quickly a friendship may develop, as long as the other party is interested in what the first child wants to do. Many children with non-verbal communication problems can do this part of friendship building because they can talk about what interests them and initially appear knowledgeable and fascinating.

However, the next stage — keeping the friendship going — depends on the child having good understanding of the role of both speaker and listener. We saw in 'Making conversations work' (see page 96) that 'sharing' means being able to ask the other children about their likes and dislikes. But it also involves being able to talk about your interest in that topic.

Children who can't share information in this manner tell you everything they know about their favourite subject because they are only confident talking about this topic and can't cope with supplementary questions. A proficient communicator — one who has well-developed non-verbal communication skills — is comfortable talking about a range of subjects and can interact well within the conversation.

Your child may be able to start up a friendship through conversation, but can she maintain it? If she hasn't the conversational skills to keep friendships

> ## TRY THIS!
>
> Another idea for helping your child to share information is to arrange play dates with her friends: they could play with construction toys, dress up, do cooking, play shops, paint or play music.
>
> These and many outdoor activities are excellent opportunities to model conversations – questioning, commenting and sharing thoughts. Encourage your child to talk with her friends about things they have done together, for example after playing on the swings at the park, when you get back to the house, go over what you have done together. Help her talk about what has happened at the park. Look for opportunities to agree, share different points of view and clarify what happened.

going, your child may become confused (because she won't understand why this is happening) or depressed because she appears to be unpopular. Children I have worked with are desperate to make friends but often just don't know how to make conversations work for them.

Help your child learn how to share information in a two-way exchange. This should happen early on as her conversations develop. The more she can practise this skill the more her interest in others will develop. Then she will start asking about what others think, feel or want to do, developing more areas of shared interest.

WILL SHE BE ABLE TO MAKE FRIENDS ON HER OWN?

Once she is able to initiate these friendship-building conversations, you can take a back seat.

WHAT CAN HAPPEN?

Here are two conversations, one of which is an example of 'sharing' and the other is not:

Fred: *'I have this amazing game of fantasy about a boy who meets a wizard and they go to a forest and in the forest the wizard gives the boy some magic powers. The boy can run like the wind and turn anything into what he wants it to be. I like this game and I have decided to develop it into a computer programme so that I can play it on my computer and then you can play it on your computer too.'*

Mark: *'What's it called?'*

Fred: *'The boy then goes home to see his mum and she says "Where have you been?" but the boy runs upstairs to try out his powers ...', etc.*

This is the second version of the conversation:

Fred: *'Hi Mark, guess what? I have developed a really good game. Would you like to hear about it?'*

Mark: *'Yes, what happens?'*

Fred: *'It's about a boy who goes into a wood and meets a wizard. He gives the boy special powers.'*

Mark: *'What powers are they?'*

Fred: *'He can run like the wind and turn anything into what he needs it to be but for only one day. Have you ever played a game like that?'*

Mark: *'I think so, but the boy became a wizard.'*

Fred: *'Well, I think that idea sounds interesting, I'll see if I can make my boy into a wizard too.'*

In the first conversation, Fred is doing all the talking and doesn't pay any attention to what Mark says. He just carries on talking regardless, not leaving opportunities for his friend to ask anything. This is not sharing information at all, this is **talking at someone**.

Mark may have initially been fascinated by what Fred is saying, but he will soon become fed up with the lack of two-way traffic. Mark may also feel that Fred is not really interested in talking to him because Fred doesn't look at children when talking to them.

In the second conversation, Fred is pausing in what he says and must be looking because he is seeking responses from Mark – he gives Mark an opportunity to ask or say something. Fred then responds to what Mark has said before adding other details that he thinks Mark might want to know.

Make sure that she is able to interest others in what she says and can show interest in what they say in turn. These skills continue to develop throughout her school life, but she needs enough confidence to make a start and you can give her that confidence.

Help her to hone these skills by talking with her about conversations that go well and reflecting on those that don't and what to do to make them better. If your child is able to hold successful conversations by the time she goes to school, she will be more likely to make and keep friends. She will also be better equipped to deal with friendships that come to a natural end and understand that new ones will begin.

BUILDING FRIENDSHIPS

Attending playgroup is an excellent way for your child to meet other children and make friends. Structured play activities, such as using building blocks, give your child shared experiences in a cooperative environment. In these types of situations she will be able to watch all sorts of different conversations, for example child to child, child to adult, adult to adult and among different people, extending the range of her experiences. Every activity presents an opportunity for conversation — learning to ask questions about how to do something, why it is being done or when it is her turn to add a piece to the puzzle, for example.

If your child is not developing friendships it could be for one of two reasons:

1. She hasn't yet developed the skill of sharing within a conversation and so you just need to help her by modelling what it is she should be doing, for example saying 'Is it my turn now?' or 'Why did you put the block in that hole?' and so on.

2. Her other non-verbal skills are not sufficiently developed to help her build her friendships. If so, modelling behaviour will not work because she will not be watching what you are demonstrating to her. You need to focus on getting her

interested in watching people and activities so that she can learn to make good sense of the clues around her.

DEALING WITH CONFLICT

One of the most important skills she will acquire through developing friendships is learning how to negotiate; this is much better than having to fight her way out of trouble. Encourage as much play as possible with children her own age so that she experiences situations where she can practise her skills of negotiation. Show her how to negotiate in family or role play situations where there is no pressure.

FOCUS POINTS

★ Take her to mother and toddler groups and encourage friends to come and play.

★ Shared activities such as baking are a great way to foster friendships and give children the chance to share and talk about what they are doing, while having fun – with a tasty reward at the end!

★ Model friendship-building conversations – asking pertinent questions, leaving gaps for the other person to talk and responding to what they say.

★ Talk through successful and unsuccessful conversations she hears – you could role play what might go better next time with a toy animal, puppets or dolls.

★ Limit time spent in front of the TV and on computers.

★ Encourage play with friends indoors and out.

RELATED SKILLS

There are some skills that are less obviously associated with communication that your child will need to have in order to make good sense of conversations and be able to participate by communicating in an effective manner. These skills include symbolic understanding, prediction, change and choosing.

SYMBOLIC UNDERSTANDING

A symbol is anything that can be used to represent an object or event. It gives us the capacity to talk about things when they are not present: words are symbols.

Being able to communicate about objects, people and situations through the use of symbols is a key human attribute. The word 'chair', for example, is a symbol that stands for any chair; its value is that it can be used to refer to most things that we sit on, from a dining chair to a garden chair through to a comfy chair. Symbols are very powerful.

The first stage in understanding symbols is for your child to learn to assimilate the common features of a 'chair', for example. To do this he must look at many real-sized versions of different chairs. You can assist him to learn words by using drawings, photos and miniature objects to represent the words. This should be happening before he learns to speak. Remember the importance of signing to your child before he can speak. Signing is another form of symbolisation

---

HOW TO DEVELOP SYMBOLIC UNDERSTANDING IN CHILDREN WITH NO SPOKEN LANGUAGE

Check that your child is able to understand all the following symbols in the developmental order given. He will need to pass through the earlier levels before using words.

1. real objects and people

2. reduced-size objects, such as a doll's tea-set

3. photos of objects and people

4. drawings of objects and people

5. miniature objects such as small animals and cars

6. pictorial symbols (pictograms) – these are generally line drawings or images representing the objects but not necessarily resembling the object; you could use available systems such as Rebus or Makaton, or draw your own

7. pictograms seen on road signs, in hospitals, swimming pools and so on

8. spoken word

9. written word

It is not possible for your child to skip the first five levels, although some might develop concurrently, so the understanding of pictorial symbols (such as those on road signs) might occur at the same time as the spoken word. Your child needs to be good at the early stages of symbolisation to start talking with meaning.

Children with non-verbal communication difficulties who can talk do not tend to have problems with symbolic language development. But some children, such as those with autism, will need a great deal of help to move up through the levels of symbolic understanding. Progression won't happen until the child is competent at each level and may also need a longer period of consolidation at the individual levels.

that will help develop his knowledge of symbols to an advanced level.

Initially he won't know the word but will recognise the object and its purpose. If every time he sees a chair you say and sign 'chair', he will learn to associate that word with the object. Alongside this, it will help if he can associate the concept of a chair with smaller doll-sized chairs and pictures, photos or drawings of different kinds of chairs. All this helps him to confirm that his idea (or concept) of a 'chair' is consistent with other people's. Try this with a variety of different nouns, such as car, dog, ball, light, stairs, and so on.

Finally, when your child is about to enter or has just entered school, he will start to recognise the written word 'chair'. This level of symbolisation is quite advanced, but in my view spoken symbols are more complex than written symbols due to the fleeting nature of speech – it is gone as soon as it is said. The fact that he can say and hear the word 'cat', for example, will reinforce his reading of the written word: c-a-t.

START AND FINISH

Throughout the toddler phase, your child must continue to learn about the sometimes quite low-key evidence that communicates the start and finish of activities. You need to tell him what he is going to do, talk about the process of the activity and identify when it is coming to an end. For example, making cakes, you might say: 'We are going to make some cakes. First we need to mix the ingredients, then cook them in the oven and then we can eat them. Let's start with a mixing bowl.' Then while each part of the process is happening, talk about what you are doing. At the end you can say 'Cooking is finished. Now it's time to eat the cakes!'

By doing this for every activity, you will ensure that your child becomes aware of the subtle beginnings and endings, which in time will evolve into recognising boundaries of all kinds. The family meal table presents plenty of opportunities to practise this. The box (right) is a brief analysis of the stages a baby or toddler could observe at the family table two or three times a day.

WATCHING THE PROCESS OF EATING A MEAL

- The table is laid with the cutlery, communicating that the meal has not yet begun.
- You can be seen preparing the meal.
- Someone gets the plates out.
- Parents call the family to the table, saying 'Time for dinner'.
- The family sit in expectation of the food arriving (many non-verbal signals from the family as they do this – excitement, boredom, delight etc).
- The food is dished out on on clean, empty plates.
- All plates are placed in front of the people waiting to eat.
- Everyone eats the food – the full plates gradually become empty and dirty.
- The dirty cutlery and empty plates are removed.
- The remaining clean spoons communicate that the meal is not yet finished.
- You are heard to say 'Time for pudding!'
- Pudding bowls are fetched from the cupboard.
- The pudding is taken out of the fridge.
- The pudding is dished out into the bowls.
- The dishes are placed in front of those waiting to eat.
- Everyone eats the pudding – at first the plates are full and gradually they become empty and dirty.
- The dirty cutlery and empty plates are removed.
- The lack of cutlery now communicates that the meal is finished.
- All the dirty items are washed up.

Without the skill to perceive and process this information, your child will be unable to recognise boundaries that indicate what type of behaviours are acceptable and those that are not. Children who cannot identify boundaries are more likely to display tantrum behaviour for a longer period of time than is usual.

PREDICTION

Does he know what is going to happen next? If your child finds prediction hard, he may just stop doing something unexpectedly or, if you are out together, may become very upset because he does not know for certain where you will be going or what he is going to do next. Later on he may become frustrated and anxious as things don't turn out the way he expected. Help his predictive skills advance and he will have a good chance of finding school life a lot easier.

WHY ARE GOOD PREDICTION SKILLS SO IMPORTANT?

Prediction is used in many different ways – but the majority of uses are for communication purposes. For instance, your partner may say 'Dinner in five minutes' and you will know that this means you need to be at the table ready to eat in five minutes. You are able to predict from what has been said to you that a meal will be ready and that you should behave accordingly.

Prediction also helps us know what messages our listener wants or needs to hear. If you are in a shoe shop, for example, you will know that the assistant does not need to be asked whether they sell bikes! From the clues of the situation – all kinds of footwear and your past knowledge of shoe shops – you will know that the assistant will respond more favourably to a question about shoes, boots or sandals. All day long we are predicting what we need to do and say in each situation.

Unable to predict

Because this girl has no idea where she is going, she is starting to have a tantrum. Her prediction skills are not sufficiently developed to pick up that they are going home for tea.

Prediction also helps us to know how to say something to the garden centre shop assistant. For example you would not cuddle up to them and whisper in their ear 'Where can I find the carrot seeds?' Neither would you shout at them in an angry way. Because you have experienced situations like this repeatedly, you know that you will stand at a friendly but not too intimate distance and speak clearly and in a matter-of-fact tone.

Prediction also tells you when to say something. You can predict that it is going to be your turn to talk from the grammar, from the content of what is being said, the stress pattern or a non-verbal signal from the speaker. There is more on how to know when it is your turn to talk in the chapter 'Making conversations work' (page 107).

We also need to predict what will happen in a given situation because, if we can't, we are likely to become anxious. Think of situations where you are unable to predict the outcome and you will realise how important prediction is to keep you confident and unstressed. For instance, if you are

applying for a new job there are levels of anxiety caused by not knowing whether you have been selected for interview or, after the interview, whether or not you have got the job. Each of these stressful situations is driven by the fact that you are unable to predict the outcome of events.

Under such stress, communication is the first thing that deteriorates and, for your child, can cause further anxiety. Also, if he hasn't developed sufficient non-verbal skills, then, unlike an adult, he will be unable to rationalise his situation by relating it to previous occasions when he experienced similar feelings.

Think of situations that you might find yourself in, for example when you see a colleague or friend at their desk looking terribly sad. By reading the situation and the body language, and comparing what you see with your previous experience, you will know that it would not be right to go up to them and say 'Did you have a great time at the party last night?' Before you even say something, your subconscious is telling you this would not elicit a good reaction and is steering you towards saying something along the lines of 'Are you feeling OK?'

IS HE ABLE TO PREDICT?
Now think about the previous two examples and relate them to a five-year-old in a classroom. His teacher is beginning to look a little stressed about a disagreement between two of the children, so your child needs to know that saying, for the tenth time, 'Johnny wants to be my friend' will not help him get the response he wants from his teacher. If he can't

predict what the teacher is thinking or feeling, the child won't know when to talk and when to keep quiet.

Also, think of situations where your five-year-old has to engage with other five-year-olds, who are usually less accommodating than adults. These situations with his peers are far more challenging than other situations that he is familiar with. In the playground things are unstructured and less predictable than at home, where bath time always comes before bedtime, or in class, where a regular timetable is followed.

Prediction is vital for good communication in many ways. Lack of prediction can produce anxiety. Here are a few things that your son needs to be able to do by the time he goes to school:

1. Evaluate the situation and know what is going on.
2. Look at his teacher.
3. Based on what he sees, combine this with his understanding of the teacher's body language.
4. Relate it to his past experiences of similar situations.
5. Predict what the teacher might be about to say.

Having a bath
This girl doesn't enjoy her bath, particularly not having her hair washed. Let's hope she settles down ready for bed after being so upset.

6. Change his behaviour accordingly to prevent his teacher from becoming angry with him.

To complicate things further, your son has only four to five years to develop all the necessary skills to achieve this. Children of his age have the potential to react or change what they are doing and feeling at a moment's notice. For instance, a game is going along nicely with everybody chasing each other around, then suddenly someone has had enough

TRY THIS!

To make sure your child is able to predict in all situations by the time he enters school:

- Continue to provide loud and clear non-verbal signs to help him notice what is going on.
- When repeating everyday activities, such as having a bath, eating lunch or going to the park, surround them by visual clues that 'shout' what is happening. For example, at bath time always start off with saying (and signing), 'It's time for bath' then take him to the bathroom, turn on the taps, take his clothes off, let him go to the toilet then get in the bath.
- All the time talk about what you are doing – 'Let's turn on the taps, whoosh, out comes the water. Is the water too hot? Is it too cold?', 'Off come your clothes, first your trousers and top, then your vest, then your pants and socks', 'Sit on the toilet. Do a wee', 'Get into the bath' and so on. (If your child is struggling with speech, please only give one word or phrase at a time for each part of the activity.)
- When you want him to concentrate for listening to a story or music, drawing a picture or doing anything else, encourage him to sit down ready. Signal this by saying something like 'Let's sit down and read a story.' Distractions such as TV, radio or computer games should be turned off.
- Model the importance of focusing on

what is happening – try not to be doing something else at the same time, for example texting on your mobile.
- If your child has a lot of energy you just need to work a bit harder to get his interest and make sure he sits still and listens.
- Continue to use visual clues to help your child know what is going to happen even when he is three or four. The more clues you use the more likely he is to recognise what is going to happen. This will hone his ability to notice and respond to the much more subtle non-verbal clues that he will need to be aware of at school entry – see more on how to use visual timetables in 'Troublesome Children' (page 134).
- Don't forget that the signals for the end of activities also need to be clear. You could use a sound such as a timer to warn of the end or start of something, or use a countdown technique: 'TV will finish when I get to 3 – 1, 2, 3. TV is finished.' If you say that you will turn it off in five minutes, be consistent and do so.
- If he shows signs of persistent problems in this area, use visual timetables to show him each activity and to signal the beginning and end of an activity.
- Accompany these visual signs with the words 'It's time for …'. and when the activity is ended, say '… is finished'. For example 'It's time for lunch' and 'lunch is finished'.

and the other children notice the change in mood. If your son fails to do this and continues to chase the other children, he may become ostracised from the group.

In the school playground, with a lot of other children running around, each playing their own idiosyncratic games with their own rule system, your child will need to spot the clues that tell him another child has had enough of being tickled or doesn't want to be told any more information about dinosaurs. Children who can't do this may be shunned by their peers.

Prediction enables us to have certainty that something will, or will not, happen. It also helps us to know that we won't be doing the same thing for ever – important if your child does not particularly enjoy what he is doing and is able to look forward to something that he does enjoy.

THE IMPORTANCE OF EXPERIENCE

The reason we become better at processing non-verbal information is simply that, each day of our life, our experiences reinforce, improve and refine our understanding of situations. So, as we get older, we are able to analyse situations quicker and more easily than younger people and for this reason can communicate more effectively.

The experiences that your toddler has each day are helping him accumulate what is known as 'experiential' information, which he will use to add to his understanding of body language, and so on. Any non-verbal clues that you can draw to his attention will help him accumulate this knowledge for himself so that he can use his experience when he is not with you.

WHAT IS CHOICE?

Choice is the ability to decide between two or more options. The capacity to deal with choice is another necessary skill for communication on many levels. Without choice your child is automatically given things and he has no need to communicate. Choosing is also an important precursor to the skill of prediction and understanding consequences. The activity of 'choosing' offers opportunities to practise asking for what he wants, telling you if he needs clarification or asking for help as well as giving information. It is a wonderful way of helping children exercise their conversational skills.

HOW DOES CHOOSING DEVELOP?

First we need to look at how to develop the skill of choosing. This will only happen when you start offering objects or activities to your child instead

TRY THIS!

1. Offer choices at a symbolic level that he can understand: real objects, small objects, photos, symbols or written words.

2. Offer choices clearly – one choice in each hand. Keep the choices clearly separated so that if he just looks to indicate his choice. It is evident which one he is choosing.

3. Use small trays if your child is finding it hard – put the choices on separate trays. This gives a frame round the objects, which some children find helpful.

4. It is important to start by offering a positive and a negative choice. For instance a pudding choice should include one that your child definitely wouldn't want to eat. Giving a choice of two things he likes does not allow you to see that he has made an active choice.

5. Be aware how easy it is to think that your child is choosing when he is not. He may have just learned the procedure and knows that you want him to take one of the items.

6. By following the steps above, you will help him to generalise this skill to other situations.

of just giving him what you think he wants in advance. It is quite simple and is achieved by offering two choices, one in each hand — for example a drink in one hand and a book in the other. Then you can say 'Drink or book? Choose'. As this is an important new skill, keep the language simple to start with. You can also use a sign for 'choose' — see below. Again, this can also be introduced when you are encouraging signs at the baby stage — see 'Coping with change' (page 57).

As with most of the things that we do all day, such as deciding on the day's activities over breakfast, talking to the postman, ringing the doctor, choosing which TV programme to watch, and so on, we depend on conversations to make satisfactory choices and get things done.

7. Next you could develop this into a choice between two puddings (or other items) he likes because you now know he can choose.

8. Choosing must include the option to reject the choices offered, otherwise it is not a genuine choice.

9. Signalling the choice or rejection of 'choice', combined with signs for choosing and rejection, is a good method of establishing this skill, for example 'You have chosen the yoghurt. You don't want the banana.'

10. A possible sign for 'choice' is to close the three middle fingers of one hand, stretch little finger and thumb away from other fingers. Move towards the object referred to, saying 'Choose', and when he has chosen, say 'Good choosing'.

11. One sign for rejection is to make a 'pushing away' movement from the stomach with the back of the hand towards the body (thumb downward). You can use another 'made up' sign as long as the same sign is used consistently to mean 'no'. You could wag your finger and say 'No, no, no' with an exaggerated tone of voice.

12. Once the skill is established, offer many choices throughout the day to ensure that your child is honing this skill and will be able to make informed choices later in life.

13. You can extend this by thinking differently about games you play with him. Set the game up so that he needs to ask or tell you something before making a move. If necessary, hold on to equipment or the card he needs and only give it when he asks — he is choosing to ask you for something.

14. Offer him a choice of two cards when playing 'Happy Families' (or other card games) and say 'Which one would you like?' Only give the card when your child asks for it — through talking or other non-verbal methods. Remember it is the skill of 'choosing' you are helping him with and not simply getting him to 'talk'.

SIGN FOR 'CHOOSE'

DEALING WITH CHANGE

Your child needs to develop strengths in understanding what change really means. Like so many areas of non-verbal conversational skill, this depends on the ability to recognise what is happening in the moment and having the opportunity to practise dealing with it.

Difficulties in dealing with change are commonly found in children, particularly those on the autistic spectrum. Many establishments make effective use of visual clues to support these children. However, if you ensure that your child's understanding of change develops at an early age, he will not need to depend on artificial visual clues and will be better able to deal with change for himself.

To recognise change he needs to be aware of beginnings and endings, and be able to predict and to interpret the situation correctly. All these communication skills are dependent on each other. Help your child recognise the signals that indicate change is about to happen: expect him to be doing this between about two and four years of age.

HOW TO INTRODUCE CHANGE

The best way to ensure your child notices change is to start by making bold signals for positive changes (for example 'We can't go to the park, so let's go swimming instead') before introducing any that might be emotionally challenging.

If he doesn't see that things are going to change start by using an exaggerated vocal clue such as, 'Whoopee' and sign 'change' (see below). Then tell him what is going to change.

With fists facing each other, hook index fingers. Twist hands round each other.

SIGN FOR 'CHANGE'

If this doesn't work try using a visual clue – a brightly coloured, luminous card in the shape of a circle or star, for instance. You want him to learn to associate this with the idea of change; so every time there is a change, show the card and say 'Time to change! Now it's time for … (say what is going to happen).'

This helps by directing his attention to the situation, and while he is watching he should see the clues that indicate a change is on the way. Remember that if he is not watching, he will not learn to identify the clues.

He will soon need to recognise other less obvious signals of change such as you getting the car keys out (indicating a trip in the car) or walking together to the bus stop (indicating a journey on the bus). This is particularly important before he enters school. Your child's level of understanding will be good if you've followed the recommendation to signal the start and finish of all activities during the baby period of development.

Making connections

This boy has no idea why he is being told that he can't play with his toys any more. He hasn't picked up the connections – the rest of his family are packing away their beach equipment, which indicates a departure from the beach.

If you haven't, don't worry, just continue to use these obvious signals for as long as necessary and bear in mind how important it is to help your child recognise positive changes first.

A CHANGE FOR THE WORSE

Next, you will need to help him to accept disappointment when there is no positive alternative available. He might need to do this often when he is older. For negative change start with 'Uh oh! Trouble!', which your child should now be familiar with from the Margaret Miller *Baby Faces* book recommended in Part Two of this book.

Then tell your child about the change to something that might not be so appealing. If this doesn't work, you can introduce a different card which says 'Oops' or 'Oh dear!' Once you are certain that he understands positive change, introduce one of these cards with a negative type of change, for example 'Oh dear, we can't go to the swings, let's go to the supermarket instead' or 'Oops, we can't go and see Granny, let's make the beds instead', insert something your child won't have chosen to do or may not wish to do.

As long as you have been drawing your child's attention to these clues, you should not need to continue in this vein for very long. However, if he has not developed the skill of recognising the beginnings and ends of activities, you will need to continue to support him by keeping the signals bold and explicit for a longer period. Use an exaggerated intonation pattern and arm movements with the 'Oh dear!' part of the message so that your child will have more visual and auditory clues to draw on in addition to the words.

Only when he has learned to cope with positive change independently will he be ready to deal with negative changes effectively – you may have to work hard to get these established as they may be difficult for him to accept.

Without this skill, he may react badly to change and this may prolong tantrums into school life. At this age you have the chance to be certain that he is able to deal with change. Here is a summary:

- Be clear about the nature of the change; start with positive change.
- Offer an alternative if possible.
- Make the change no less interesting to your child than the activity being cancelled.
- Help him deal with negative changes.

Once you are sure that your child is able to recognise different types of change and react to them positively, you can be confident he will be better able to cope at school, moving easily from class to playground or class to assembly etc.

'RULES'

Here you will see how the rules your child learns will also help him cope in different areas of school. Here we look at the unspoken 'rules' we apply to many different situations and specifically those rules that make a conversation work.

Whenever we go into situations as adults we apply unspoken rules about how to behave in that situation. For example, when attending a training session, participants know from previous experience to sit and listen to the person who is deemed to be the 'trainer' and not to fire a barrage of questions at them before the subject has even been introduced.

Your child needs to accumulate 'rules of behaviour' from what he observes, from what adults tell him, and from his own experience. These rules tell him both how to communicate and what behaviour is expected in different situations, for example how to behave in cinemas, when queuing, in a library or church, on a bus or a train.

You can help him acquire knowledge of what works and what doesn't so that he will develop the ability to use these 'rules' effectively for himself. For example, if you tell him to say his brother's name when he wants to attract his attention, rather than hitting him on the arm, the next time he wants to talk to his brother he might try saying his name. If this gets a positive response he will then use this approach with other people to see if they also respond to their name. If he continues to hit people to attract their attention, remind him about the better way to achieve this.

Also, if he notices that, when his parents are speaking, they don't both speak at the same time, your child should learn not to interrupt. If this gets a good reaction in a few situations, the rule becomes confirmed and verified. It is very important for you to notice when he has applied a rule correctly and praise him — you could say 'Good waiting' or 'Good sitting still', depending on the circumstances.

Think of all the 'rules' your child will require in his 'database' in order to behave as expected on school entry. As long as you have been developing all the non-verbal skills necessary, you should only have to encourage and monitor him in applying the correct rules to situations.

Interpretation is at the heart of this skill: unless he correctly identifies what carries the meaning in a situation, he won't be able to speculate on the appropriate communication or behaviour. This is something that becomes increasingly valuable as life goes on, especially at school.

CONNECTING AND GENERALISATION

The ability to associate different experiences, to move from one situation to another connecting relevant aspects, or to see connections within a given activity, are important aspects of learning. Your child needs to be able to apply what he has learned to new situations — that he can eat an apple in the car or coming out of the swimming pool as well as at the table, for example. If he learns that apples are eaten only at the table he will not apply this to other situations.

Although children diagnosed on the autistic spectrum find this aspect of communication very difficult, it is possible to encourage generalisation by improving their interpretational skills. The more severely impaired autistic child will find it hard to generalise very basic skills, such as having a drink or going to the toilet, and will do things in unexpected locations without any idea that it might be the wrong place. Other people might interpret this as the child 'choosing' to misbehave or simply 'winding up' others. The child is definitely not doing this.

Behaviour in public
The boy on the right hasn't learned how to behave when he is out with his family because he is poor at picking up clues to help him generalise from one situation to another. Look at the distress on the faces of his mum and brother because they don't know how to change his behaviour.

In an educational context, children find the lack of generalisation a huge impediment. Your child will use this ability in many areas of his school life, from recognising and adapting to the daily routine to knowing that colouring can be applied when doing art, geography or maths; or that despite the class being moved to the music room, the subject will still be maths. A child who depends on the familiar indicators of a maths lesson such as the usual room, and cannot translate other signs of a maths lesson to a different location, will be very restricted academically and socially.

Your child needs to be able to identify and focus on the important clues in a situation and then use those to help him make connections in new situations. Once he can apply something learned in one context and use it effectively in another, you can be sure that his ability to generalise is developing. For example:

- he sees that putting his toys away in the living room makes you happy
- so he puts his toys away in his bedroom to see if that makes you happy too.

By interpreting the relevant clues, your child will be able to use his experience to guide his responses in the future and in a variety of circumstances.

SPECULATION

Your child needs to be willing and able to have a go at guessing for many aspects of communication. He needs to do this in order to learn what people might be talking about. If he just says 'I don't know' all the time, he won't get the opportunity to share things with you that will help him make a better judgement about what people are saying, their intentions and their feelings.

He will also need to speculate when deciding which behaviour or communication style to apply in any given circumstance. We subconsciously evaluate each scene by processing non-verbal signals from the people present, reading clues from the situation or context and comparing these with our experience. Our behaviour is based on this assessment, and how we behave depends on how accurate the assessment is.

The ability to consider options and alternatives, and to speculate about possible scenarios, helps us refine our choices and select the behaviour that suits the situation. This derives from our experience and ability to make connections between situations.

I have found that speculation is a skill that is poorly developed in many children. Consequently, when asked what they think is going on in a situation they often come up with a completely unexpected answer. See box, What can happen?, page 132, for an example of what can happen if a child gets it

WHAT CAN HAPPEN?

A child sees other children in the playground and decides to join in because he thinks that it is playtime. He hasn't noticed that they are in teams, that they are wearing different coloured tops, that the game is organised by the teacher and that the bell hasn't gone for playtime. Nor has he taken into account that he is on his way to another lesson or the toilet and not yet going out to play.

A child at primary school should be capable of collating a wide range of clues to correctly interpret what is going on. Even if he hasn't had experience of seeing children playing netball, there are enough signs to tell him that this is not playtime.

Ahoy, m' captain!
This boy is learning how to pretend. He is dressing up as a pirate, using a toilet roll as a telescope. As long as his mum and dad are sure he knows this is pretend, he will do well!

wrong. If children are unable to think of different explanations for what they see, their responses will be limited. For their behaviour and communication to be in tune with the circumstances they need to be able to review a range of explanations and choose the 'best' (most likely) option.

The same applies to conversations — we adjust our behaviour as we go along and as we receive more information. If your child hasn't developed the skill of analysis and speculation based on what he can see or hear, he may be limited to a false interpretation and not know how to respond as others expect him to. Talk to your child about a range of different situations that you are both familiar with and ask him to guess what might be going to happen. Also talk about which options might be best.

FANTASY VERSUS REALITY

From an early age your child will have to learn the difference between reality and fantasy because this is important later in his life — knowing which

things on the TV are real and which are fiction, for example. Starting to learn the difference between reality and 'pretend' life at an early age will help him learn the differences between real and fictional stories in books and on the TV.

This is why 'let's pretend' games used to be a major part of childhood: they are an easy way of learning about fantasy. Remember everything I have said about the obvious signalling of activities and apply it here. Your child must learn the signals associated with 'pretend' play. For example, from early on (about 12 months or so) start to say 'Let's pretend this spoon is a stick and this tin is a drum.' You could make up a sign for 'pretend' or use the one below from Cath Smith's book on signing for early years.

Be aware that, until your child is very good at knowing when something is real or not, it is unwise to let him watch films or TV that are fantasy based. This is a very good reason for not letting young children see films outside their age certification. Your child may totally misinterpret what is happening as being safe and try to emulate it himself, with potentially dangerous consequences.

Tip of extended middle finger touches nose, then hand moves and twists to point forward and down.

SIGN FOR 'PRETEND'

- Help him to answer such questions from his own perspective – to do this effectively you may need to question others or check his playgroup diary or home-school book.

- To develop his experience for use later in his life, encourage him to join in all the things that you do in and outside the home.

- Help him to make choices where he fully understands what is going on.

- Signal changes very clearly – start with exaggerated words and sounds, such as 'Uh oh!' or 'Oops' then use visual clues to help him recognise positive changes and draw his attention to negative ones.

- Help him practise his rules by repeatedly modelling what he should do in situations that are new to him.

- Encourage him to use these rules in new or different situations.

- Help him to see the connections between situations, comment on the clues that tell you that you're in the kitchen rather than the bathroom, for example.

- Encourage guessing – it doesn't matter if he is wrong! Tell him what your guess would be.

- Play 'let's pretend' with miniature objects such as tea-sets or toy animals.

- Check to make sure he can draw conclusions in situations, at the doctor, in the shoe shop etc.

- Repeat all these points, if necessary, as often as required.

FOCUS POINTS

- Look through picture books with real photos or drawings and talk to your child about what is going on.

- Help him recognise objects or people in photos or drawings.

- Be clear about clues telling him when things 'start' and 'finish', drawing his attention to the 'start' and 'finish' of activities, for instance 'Bath is finished' or 'Time for walk'.

- Help him predict what people might say, think and feel.

- Model how to ask others about themselves, for example 'What have you been doing today?'

TROUBLESOME CHILDREN

We have already seen that if you promote good interpretation and communication, your child's behaviour will improve as a consequence of her being less frustrated by circumstances; she will have a better understanding of what is happening around her and be more capable of controlling events — through communication rather than poor behaviour. Here are some other ways of improving your child's behaviour, as well as some things to avoid!

USE OF PICTURES, SYMBOLS AND SIGNS

Your child will benefit tremendously from the use of picture clues as an indication of what is happening now, is going to happen or has previously happened. If you are having trouble with her difficult behaviour or tantrums, setting up a visual timetable will help structure your child's day in a way that she will be able to understand.

You can draw these or take photos of objects and activities that make sense to your child and are of things she will be doing during the day, including breakfast, toilet, cleaning teeth, tidying the room, washing up, making the bed, going home, having a drink.

Try to think of the beginnings and ends of all the things that your child does during the day and make pictures to represent them. Eating her lunch, for example, can be divided into all these aspects with start and finishes: (1) in high chair, (2) bib, (3) full plate, (4) main course, (5) drink, (6) pudding, (7) wash face and hands, (8) lunch finished, (9) out of high chair.

When introducing these picture clues to her begin with only one

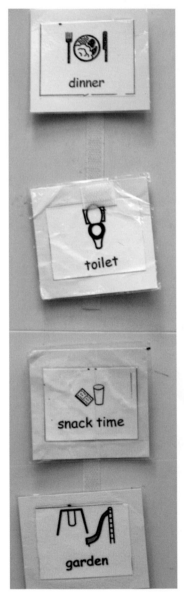

card at a time, then gradually introduce more. Once she knows two or three cards you can start to put them in sequences for the morning or afternoon — 'breakfast', 'clean teeth', 'read story' for instance. This is her 'timetable'.

Write the word underneath the picture so all the people who use the cards with her use the same word to describe the activity, and laminate the cards or cover them in sticky-back clear plastic. It's a good idea not to make the cards too big as you may want to take them with you for use outside the home. You could make a holder for the cards — this could be a photo wallet or one that you make as a strip, here is an example of one used in a school local to me.

As indicated elsewhere in this book, use each card at the start of an activity, saying 'It is time for toilet'. At the end of the activity say 'Toilet is finished. It's time for a story'. As long as she is looking, the use of these cards draws your child's attention to the non-verbal signals that tell us when things start and finish. Draw her attention to these clues if she doesn't notice for herself.

Have a 'finished' place, perhaps a wallet, bag or basket, so your child can mark the end of each activity by putting the card in the wallet after you have told her that '… is finished'. Then at the end of the morning or afternoon, you can take the cards out and, in the order of the activities, talk about each thing your child has done during the session. Encourage her to help you set up the next sequence of activities. Don't forget to give her choices of what she wants to do and the order in which they will happen. The joy of using these timetables is that the more your child has control of the process the better it will be for the development of her communication. You are trying to help her use communication to control her day-to-day life in an acceptable way. Without this ability she may resort to behaviour which, as she becomes older and larger, will be more and more difficult for you to deal with.

If you need to use supports such as visual timetables with your child, it will be because she is struggling to make sense of the world. Please be consistent in your communication and if the 'timetable' says it is time for a story, then read a story! Your child's confusion will be made worse if you insist on her finishing putting the shopping away when she is expecting a story. Pictorial symbols and clues are there to tell your child what

is happening, so if you do something different she will not develop the necessary skills, and may become frustrated and resort to unacceptable behaviour to vent this.

Remember how important signing is for your child, especially if speech is late developing. When you teach her signs include nouns, verbs and adjectives (page 106) so that she will be able to put these words together to make longer phrases and sentences.

There are many books of signs, but I recommend those that make use of British Sign Language (BSL) as these are based on the day-to-day signs used by deaf people and are more practical than systems based on language development. There are good books on these signs for children by Cath Smith,

TRY THIS!

These ways of talking to your child will work because they don't overload her with spoken language that exacerbates her confusion.

1. Use positive messages: try to say things in a manner that reinforces what you want her to do. So, instead of 'Don't splash in the bath', say 'Keep still in the bath.' The result is the same but achieved in a positive style. There are two reasons for this:

- You want to keep negative expressions for really serious issues, and if throughout the day 50 per cent of your interactions are negative, your child is less likely to 'hear' the negative message when you really need her to.
- Young children are only able to listen to one or two words in a sentence. So if you have to use a negative, make the sentence simple. For instance, if you say 'We aren't going swimming', your child might just hear 'swimming' and

interpret it as a positive message, ie 'going swimming'! In this case you shouldn't be surprised if you get a behaviour outburst when she doesn't get to go swimming. Instead, say 'No swimming' (sign 'No' to really draw attention to th negative). You can repeat this until you are certain that she understands.

- Children don't fully learn to understand complex negatives until nearer school entry age. So my advice is to keep all messages that are given to or in front of your child positive for as long as possible, and by school age her understanding of negatives should be good.

2. Remember that sarcasm and innuendo are far too difficult, so avoid these wherever possible and if you do find yourself using them, please just explain the meaning in clear terms to your child (see 'Hidden meanings', page 81).

including her *Let's Sign Pocket Dictionary*, which has more than 1,000 signs.

HOW TO TALK TO YOUR CHILD

Be clear and specific when you talk to your child so she understands what you are saying and can use it to change or adapt her behaviour the next time a similar situation occurs.

Keep your language short and sweet. Don't embellish what you say with social niceties such as 'Would you mind …?' or 'Wouldn't it be nice if …?' We often tend to dress things up to sound more 'polite'. Your child is learning how to communicate and the easiest way for her to do this is to keep things very clear and simple. You can introduce the social niceties once she has learned how to understand the non-verbal messages!

INFORMATION-CARRYING WORDS

At this time her understanding of spoken language will also be developing, so knowing about what speech and language therapists call 'information-carrying words' is important. These are the words within a message that you need to understand in order to comply with the request. For example, if I say 'Please will you **sit** at the table ready for **dinner**' you only need to understand one or at most two words to know what is required – as long as there is a table in the room! I have underlined the likely words that would communicate this message effectively (ie the information-carrying words).

If you say 'I want you to …' and repeat it ten or twenty times a day, your child can focus on the meaningful word or words. Those first four words can be ignored.

HOW BEST TO PRAISE HER

We all know that praise is a key way to get a child to do what you want her to do. We hope that she will learn to use the praised behaviour in future without having to be told. However, the way you praise her is also an important factor in whether or not she understands how you want her to behave. Just saying 'Well done!' or 'What a good girl' is unlikely to achieve this as she may not know which specific behaviour you are referring to.

Imagine your child has had a bad morning; she has done many things that annoy you: spilling her drink or food, hitting out at her brother or sister, shouting at you or other adults, not doing what you have asked and so on. Then suddenly she does something that you are really pleased about. If you then say in a non-specific way 'Really well done, Joanne' or even 'That was good, Joanne', it will take a very high level of non-verbal processing for your child to know which particular behaviour you are praising her for and would like her to repeat. However, if you are very specific and use this method of praising, she will know what you are referring to – 'Good waiting, Jo' or 'Good listening, Jo' – because you name the action or activity that has pleased you.

INFORMATION GIVING

Effective communication includes having some idea of what your listener knows or what they don't know. This is bound up with her understanding

of 'shared knowledge' (see 'Who am I?' on page 93 for more).

If your child is only able to talk about what she wants to talk about, others will find her hard to communicate with, or will tire of talking to her. Encourage her to talk about things that are relevant to those present and the situation.

Start by getting her to tell you what she sees going on when you are with her, so you know that what she tells you is relevant. If she can't do this, tell her what you think is going on and point out the clues that help you draw this conclusion, for example 'I see Granny going to the shed with her boots on. I think she is going to do some gardening now.'

Another way of helping to improve information giving is to get your child to tell you what people

Children giving good information
These two girls are having a 'pretend' party and are chatting away just like they have seen their parents doing.

are talking about. To help her, explain that people usually talk about what they are doing: when eating a meal, for example, they talk about the food, when driving in the car they talk about where they are going, or when getting the bath ready and turning on the taps they might talk about the toys they want in the bath. This is just a starting point for your child. Once she recognises all the non-verbal clues – who it is, what they are wearing and so on – she will be able to start talking about a range of topics.

In order to tell whether she is able to talk relevantly about things of which you have no knowledge, you need some sense that what she says is usually accurate. If you start by asking her to tell you things you don't know about, for example what she did when she went to play at her friend's house, it will be more difficult to verify what she says.

Sometimes, your child may not realise that her listener has heard enough about a particular topic and she will carry on regardless. See 'Try this!' on page 137 for a way of helping her to see that too much information, or too little, can be problematic and then to learn how she can give people just the right amount.

Check frequently that what she says is on target and at the right level. The more you practise this with her, the more confidence she will gain in making conversations relevant when on her own.

USING BOOKS TO PROMOTE
CONVERSATIONAL SKILLS

Books are a really good way of helping your child to communicate more effectively. Instead of reading what is written, look at the pictures and ask her to tell you what she thinks is going on, what the people might be thinking, saying or feeling, or what they are about to do.

A good set of books to do this with is the Oxford Reading Tree. Choose the stories that are about everyday activities, not the fantasy stories, and talk about the pictures in the manner advised. A good place to start might be Oxford Reading Tree, *Read with Biff, Chip, and Kipper*, Level 1.

These books are not ideal because they are drawings of people rather than photographs, but the drawings are very good and an adequate substitute. You will also have to cover the words so your child cannot read them because most

children with non-verbal conversational difficulties are good readers. You want to encourage her to get the sense from the visual clues found in the pictures.

Other books with just pictures and no words are more difficult to find and tend not to cover everyday topics. A good idea is to make up your own stories using photo sequences of activities and situations your child comes across regularly.

Books are also helpful for developing a wide range of conversational skills – you can talk about the stories, characters and scenes that you are reading together. She will also be able to practise asking questions, saying what she thinks and making observations and comparisons.

Many games can also be adapted to encourage your child to ask about the process of the game or predict what might be going to happen and so on.

Look, Mum, they're making a sandcastle!
This child is enjoying sharing information about the book with her mum. She will hear her mum telling her what she can see and making comments on what she says. She will be expanding her vocabulary and conversational skills at the same time.

You may just need to look at them from a different perspective. (See how to play 'Guess Who?' in 'Making conversations work', page 109.)

WHAT TO AVOID

You might have read or been told about using a 'naughty step' or 'time-out' to benefit your child when you are finding her behaviour problematic. The use of the 'naughty step' has come into vogue in recent years and is a good tactic in a parent's repertoire, but for a child with limited non-verbal understanding it is not a good method of improving behaviour. It is only of use if her ability to understand non-verbal messages is equal to her understanding of the spoken word.

You are probably expecting her to make the connection between the 'punishment' and the behaviour, so she will learn not to repeat it. However, there is a risk that your child will not understand what she is being punished for as she may not be able to pick up unspoken or other non-verbal clues pinpointing the 'naughty' behaviour.

If your child cannot make the connection, she will spend time on the 'naughty step' and may even learn to say 'sorry' afterwards, but she won't link this to her behaviour, that is the reason she was sent to the naughty step in the first place. Saying 'sorry' may give you the impression that she has made the connection, but it is more likely to be simply a learned response because she wants to please you. When she repeats the behaviour in a week or two, you may think she has chosen to ignore the lesson and behave badly when in fact she didn't make the connection on the previous occasion, so doesn't know how you want her to behave.

Another reason for not using 'time-out' or the 'naughty' step is that it is a 'punishment'. For more positive ways on handling this behaviour, see the 'When you are ready to talk' strategy in the 'Try this!' box under 'Tantrums' in the chapter 'What should I look out for?', page 144.

If you have to use a 'naughty step', give her a visual reminder of why she has been sent there. You could make some cards that cover most situations when you might feel it necessary to send her to the step, for example hitting a sibling, throwing toys

or food, arguments about watching TV, and so on. Visual reminders will help her remember why she was sent to the step and therefore provide a clear link to the behaviour. Children with poor non-verbal skills are also less able to ask for help, so you shouldn't expect her to come and say 'Why did you send me to the naughty step?' Using the visual prompts means that she has a better chance of asking about what she has done to upset you.

FOCUS POINTS

★ Use 'timetables' to help your child know what is going on and what to talk about.

★ Make the symbolic level right for her – picture, sign, symbol, etc.

★ Too many words will only confuse your child.

★ Keep your language clear and simple.

★ Keep messages as positive as you can.

★ Indicate by opening up your hands if she gives too much information or bringing them close together if she gives too little.

★ Use picture story books to help her work out what people are doing or are going to do, or what they are thinking, feeling or saying.

★ Books are a good way of helping her to talk about different topics and practise different ways of speaking – questions, answers, giving details, etc.

★ Be specific when praising.

★ Try not to use the 'naughty step' or 'time out' – effective use of these depends on your child having excellent non-verbal understanding.

WHAT SHOULD I LOOK OUT FOR?

The purpose of this book has been to ensure that your child grows up with all the necessary communication skills. If you have been following the advice so far, he shouldn't be having any problems with making good use of his conversational skills in everyday life. However, it is possible that he will show signs of weakness in some areas. In that case, go back to the appropriate chapter and revisit the advice.

How do you know if your child is having problems associated with a lack of non-verbal communication skills? Children who have difficulty holding effective conversations adopt strategies to get out of a conversation they are finding confusing. Your child may do any of the following:

- dominate conversations by talking only about what interests him
- opt out of conversations by physically leaving the vicinity – running to his room or some other place of safety
- become aggressive or inappropriate with his language – he might start swearing or being verbally abusive
- be physically aggressive when people continue to talk to him, failing to recognise that he finds conversation confusing.

If he behaves in any of these ways, use the strategies described later in this chapter.

SIGNS THAT HE MIGHT BE STRUGGLING
Here is a list of indicators that you need to look for in your child. Any of these signs may be a signal that you need to change the way you communicate with your child and start helping him develop his conversational skills.

- He isn't interested in faces, or he looks at people occasionally when talking or listening but doesn't notice their interest (or lack of it).
- He starts talking before he is one year old. In this case you must check that he has all the skills in Part One of this book and if he hasn't, start doing more nursery rhymes or talk to him in a simpler, clearer fashion and encourage his interest in faces.
- He quickly becomes very good at talking. This might include developing an extra large vocabulary around one topic that is not very useful in day-to-day life, for example dinosaurs, cars, fantasy games, TV programmes.
- He talks a great deal and doesn't allow others to say anything.
- He gives only one- or two-word responses or stops talking in all or some situations.
- He can't cope with you asking him questions.
- He might be startled or upset when things change.
- He finds sharing or playing with other children too hard and carries on preferring to play alone beyond his first year.
- His behaviour changes suddenly for no apparent reason.
- He does things that you can't explain.
- As he gets older he doesn't show interest in other toddlers but tends to go to adults when he wants something.
- He panics at being left with strangers – at a playgroup or childminder's, for example.
- He suddenly gets very angry for no apparent reason.
- He appears to be overactive and some might even think he is hyperactive. However, children who fail to learn that you need to be still to communicate effectively stop being overactive when they develop this skill!
- He doesn't like sharing books or games and finds board games very difficult.
- He fails to understand the rules of peer games and as a result might become physically aggressive.
- He hits other children, adults or objects regularly.
- He begins to self-harm.
- He doesn't participate in the two-way process of conversations.
- He is unable to report relevant details about situations of conflict.
- He is not good at taking turns in a conversation.
- He has few friends and by the time he enters

school may be aware of his isolation from his age group.

- He finds it hard to talk to children his own age and may prefer to talk to adults or children younger than himself.
- He finds telling you about events or asking about what you have been doing almost impossible.
- His intonation may be monotonous or idiosyncratic — he might develop an American or Australian accent unexpectedly.
- His facial expression doesn't vary much and can look bland.
- He opts out of conversations by running away, hiding, putting his hood or a blanket over his head.
- He chooses to talk in some situations but opts out of others (professionals may refer to this as elective or selective mutism).
- He distracts you or tries to talk to you when you are speaking to others or on the phone.
- He becomes verbally aggressive or abusive.
- He has difficulty applying a skill learned in one situation to another.
- He says things that surprise you to strangers, police or teachers etc.

If he shows any of these symptoms you need to question whether or not his non-verbal understanding has developed to a level where he can communicate well in all situations most of the time.

BE AWARE

If your child opts out of some communication situations and you think he is just 'shy', it might be that he is good at giving information at home and this ability diminishes only when he is in new or different situations. Any sign that your child's communication is different from one situation to the next must not be disregarded. You can help him by making sure his interpretation skills are really well developed and that he can read the body language and facial expressions of people other than just his family.

One mother told me that it was only when she saw her child on video trying to give the information requested in my assessment that she realised how limited his communication was outside the family home. The school had been pointing out his difficulties but because he was more confident at home and appeared to talk well, his mother thought he was simply choosing not to do so at school.

Before concluding that your child is shy or reticent, you should confirm that he is capable of processing non-verbal information in all situations.

WHAT CAN HAPPEN?

The Williams family noticed that their son wanted to control conversations most of the time and did this by constantly telling people all he knew about his different interests. Because he overloaded them with details about his favourite topic, it brought their attention to his difficulty and they began to question the cause of his behaviour. By making sure he could identify the beginning and end of information and that he understood what information is relevant to situations, they were able to develop his non-verbal skills so that he no longer needed to control conversations in this way – and he became a good listener too.

The Stuarts too realised that their daughter was controlling the conversation, but in a completely different and less demanding way. She basically avoided communication wherever possible and, as this caused few problems, her difficulties were not identified. The school found her a model pupil because she caused no disruption. However, what everyone missed was that she was not choosing to opt out because she was shy but because she felt confused in conversational situations. Everyone was then surprised when her behaviour deteriorated badly in the last stages of primary school.

TANTRUMS

Everyone knows about the 'terrible twos' when children are prone to tantrums, but few people understand why this happens at this particular time. Here you will find out what causes these behaviour problems and what you can do to prevent them occurring. If your child has poor non-verbal communication skills beyond this age, tantrums are likely to persist.

My first experience of seeing a 14-year-old lying on the floor kicking and screaming was what prompted me to come up with a programme to help children who lacked non-verbal skills to acquire them. By following this advice you will prevent a prolonged period of tantrums in your child. It is quite usual for children to have periods of obstinate anger or outbursts of frustration at around the age of two. This behaviour arises from the fact that your child's spoken language skill temporarily outstrips his non-verbal ability. As your toddler begins to speak in short phrases and sentences, others may start to think he is a better communicator than he really is.

He is probably not as competent as he sounds and is still having difficulty making sense of complicated visual information and other signals. He is able to speak but is unable to understand what is being said to him with the same facility and his ability to interpret and predict from the non-verbal information available to him is lagging behind his other communication skills.

This is no different from growth spurts, for example – not all aspects of a child's development progress at the same pace and they often proceed in short bursts. However, if there is a prolonged delay in the development of his non-verbal skills, he will continue to exhibit tantrum behaviour.

You may think that the cause of a tantrum, perhaps when out shopping, is your denying him what he wants. However, it is more likely to be a combination of some or all of the following:

- He is feeling stressed and anxious because he would rather go to the swings than go clothes shopping.
- He fails to fully understand something that has been said to him in the previous five or ten minutes – too much spoken language from adults often overloads toddlers' processing skills in stressful situations.
- He struggles to make good sense of what is going on. At home in a relaxed play situation he might have been able to understand complex phrases, but out in the real world, which is unpredictable, busy and noisy, he becomes overwhelmed.

Tantrum – fairy on the grass

There are so many factors why this girl is having a tantrum: there has obviously been a lot of expectation about the party put on her because of the effort her parents have made with her costume; she has found something at the party distressing; and, to get away from it, she lay down on the grass and is crying and shutting her eyes so she can no longer be communicated with!

- He has difficulty predicting the outcome of the current situation. He is unlikely to realise it will come to an end soon, recognise what usually happens or know where you might be taking him next.
- He does not have the ability to negotiate a better outcome — this frustration with not being able to communicate as effectively as he thinks he can spills out in anger or shouting as he tries to make his voice heard.
- He has yet to develop the ability to perceive that you are stressed, to empathise with your feelings, and be less demanding.

As he doesn't yet have the combination of verbal and non-verbal skills to deal with a situation that is tedious or challenging for him — such as being out visiting relatives for a long time or when asked to do something he doesn't want to do — he resorts to screaming and shouting, kicking or hitting out at people or objects.

WHAT CAN HAPPEN?

The Stuart family found that their toddler was not happy going round the supermarket. He would scream and shout if they went past the section that he liked to look at. This screaming would not stop until after they left the shop and were on their way home. The Stuarts started to use a 'carrot' type strategy, that is 'If you are good until we get to the car, then I will buy you sweets.' Initially this worked and after a few trips they felt the problem was solved.

But the behaviour began to return, slowly at first and within a few more trips it was back to the same volume and disruption level. In frustration they employed a 'stick'-type strategy, such as 'If you don't behave nicely, you will not watch TV when we get home.'

This certainly didn't work and soon they were resorting to carrying a screaming toddler out of the supermarket shouting and struggling while being watched by the other customers. The family became very stressed as a result and there were arguments between the parents about how to sort the problem out. They asked their extended family and nothing anyone said worked for more than a few occasions. The Stuarts always found themselves back at square one, with few options.

The Williams family were less likely to experience this behaviour because they had followed the advice about ensuring their toddler could sign. This meant that when things became difficult he could quickly communicate what he wanted. They also used visual reminders about what was going to happen in the supermarket and afterwards.

As soon as a temper tantrum began at the supermarket, all they had to do was say 'When you are ready we will talk' (see page 144) and wait for their child to calm down. Because they had used this strategy over and over again in other less stressful situations, the strategy kicked in and worked automatically when it came to the more challenging scenario of a supermarket. Once their little boy had calmed down, they could find out what he wanted and then communicate in a calm and reasonable fashion whether or not he could have his own way. To their surprise, just knowing that they wouldn't be long and that straight after they would be going home was often sufficient to calm him down completely.

Perhaps your child will have temper tantrums as a result of not knowing that it is time for TV to stop and dinner to begin because he has not spotted the clues that signal the beginnings and ends of activities. Continue to signal the end of one activity clearly by saying 'TV is finished' and then adding 'It's time for dinner.' Keep on saying the same words until it is clear that he understands what you are saying. Changing the way you say this to something like 'Hurry up now, it's time for tea' will overload his processing skills and may result in more frustration.

A child who reacts or talks in a way that is at odds with your interpretation may be experiencing difficulty putting the signals together. Don't jump to the conclusion that he is choosing to behave badly just to wind you up. Think how he may have misunderstood what was going on and you will see that his behaviour is in accordance with his understanding and, as such, makes sense to him. Explain to him the particular clues that led you to interpret a situation as you do.

HOW YOU SHOULD REACT

A tantrum is, in effect, your child's strategy to get himself out of the conversation – so talking to him is only likely to make matters worse! Use the strategy described in 'Try this!' (right). This strategy is not a punishment and should never be used as one. It is designed to give your child space to enable him to clear his head and come back to the family or conversation better able to communicate.

If your little boy goes to his room as a result of the 'When you are ready to talk' strategy, you could establish a corner there that he likes. Maybe this could have a large cushion where he can play with toys that don't require him to use language, for example squeezy toys or picture books (without any words). Or he might like to listen to or play music (not story-telling CDs), or do some drawing or colouring. These are all what are known as 'right brain' activities, which help relax his 'left brain' (the language centre) and clear his mind for communication purposes. They will also help reduce his temper.

TRY THIS!

- Stop talking immediately. It is often the talking that has confused him.
- No one else should talk to him – sisters and brothers should be kept out of the way.
- After a pause, say 'When you are ready we will talk'.
- Keep asking him 'Are you ready to talk?' You need to judge how long to leave it, but initially you should do it at least every 20–30 seconds.
- Only if he replies 'Yes' do you start talking to him again.

If you use this consistently – don't give up after one or two tries – then you should find that your child very quickly says 'I'm ready' when you ask. This is because:

- He is the only person who can bring himself back from the confusion he feels.
- You are communicating to him that you will not overload him with more speech that will confuse him further, and this gives him confidence to return to the conversation.

WHAT YOU SHOULD DO IF THE TANTRUMS PERSIST

If your child has continued to have tantrums beyond the 'terrible two' phase, it means that his non-verbal communication skills are still not keeping pace with his spoken language and, therefore, you should focus entirely on promoting the non-verbal interpretational skills recommended earlier in this book.

If your child goes to school still having tantrums, he will find himself at odds with his teacher and with the school system. Children who demonstrate these problems are at risk of being excluded – even at primary level!

STRANGER DANGER

A particular benefit of your child's increasing awareness of non-verbal signals is that he will develop the ability to distinguish between friends and strangers. If at the age of three or four your child is happy to go up to strangers and tell them all about your family or what happens at home, you should take this as a warning that his skills are not sufficiently developed and you need to pay detailed attention to the steps in 'Interpretational skills' (pages 18, 70).

Some years ago I was very concerned about a girl I was treating; her non-verbal awareness was very poor and she was unable to tell the difference between people she knew and those she didn't. Moreover, when she was unable to understand what people were saying to her, her only response was to say 'yes' and smile at people.

This became more problematic in her teenage years as it was expected that she would be safe travelling to college alone on trains or buses. You can imagine that if she used her strategy of smiling and saying 'yes' to strangers she would be very vulnerable.

To develop this essential life skill, your child needs to be able to:

- tell the difference between a friend and a stranger
- understand what is appropriate to say to people he doesn't know
- communicate in a range of styles according to the situation.

The more skilled a child is in interpreting non-verbal information, the more capable he will become with regard to dealing with strangers on his own.

CHILDREN WITH MORE COMPLEX NEEDS

Children can have non-verbal communication problems whether or not they are able to speak. Here I will talk about some things that can happen if your child has a communication problem associated with other difficulties, such as a learning disability, or has no spoken language at all.

It is extremely important that you go back to the techniques advocated for pre-talking babies at the beginning of this book if any of the following

Stranger danger
Learning not to talk to strangers is so important. Help your child develop the skills necessary to help her know the difference between friends and strangers.

applies to your child:

- he has no spoken language
- he is able to talk only by repeating what others say
- he talks only in learned phrases or stories
- he is able to say a word only when prompted to talk, for example 'Your hat goes on your...'.

If other factors impede their communication development, whatever the age, children need to start at the low-level non-verbal skills in the 'Check this' box (right). To focus on language development alone will be detrimental to the progress of conversational skills.

Shy boy hides between his mother's legs
This young boy is almost distraught because he is confused about the situation he finds himself in.

WHAT HAPPENS ON SCHOOL ENTRY?

In this chapter you will see what will be expected communicatively of your child on entry to primary school in the UK and why you need to help her be prepared. In the UK and some other countries, children enter school as young as four years of age. In the rest of Europe, school entry is often at six years, or even seven in some Scandinavian countries, and these children do no worse and many do even better academically than children in the UK.

Following the rapid and extensive development of non-verbal communication skills in the toddler phase of childhood, entry to school will determine whether your child has sufficient skills to deal confidently with day-to-day events. Only if she has developed all the skills described in this book will she be able to cope when she starts at primary school and have the foundation for further development well into her teens.

The pre-school curriculum in the UK has also changed to include targets for developing computer skills in children of three to five years of age! As you have already seen in this book, screen-based activities such as the computer or TV are detrimental to your child's ability to learn non-verbal conversational skills. If your child has learned to communicate well, then she will find using a computer very easy. This does not have to happen before she goes to school. This view is supported by many professionals who specialise in early years development — see www.earlychildhoodaction.com.

At the age of four most children do not have sufficient non-verbal skills to be confident communicators when they find themselves in new situations. This applies particularly to boys, who find developing non-verbal understanding harder than girls.

With fewer opportunities than previous generations had to develop skills, due in part to the prevalence of TV and computer use in childhood, children are now less likely to achieve their potential on school entry.

Once your child enters school, the pressure is on to develop reading and writing skills, often to the detriment of non-verbal communication. The pressure to read and write can often be too much, with the result that behaviour problems become apparent and, as many schools currently find it hard to prevent this happening, children end up on a slippery slope towards exclusion. No parent wants that for their child. However, if you have focused on promoting her conversational skills, this will stand her in good stead and improve her chances of reaching her full potential.

Many practitioners and research studies recognise that children's communication skills are now lower on school entry. In my experience, once children can talk reasonably well, schools show less concern for the development of communication. While teachers are aware of the consequences of social, emotional and behavioural problems, they may overlook the root cause of these problems, which lies in underdeveloped non-verbal communication skills.

PRIMARY SCHOOL

Teachers are sometimes baffled about why children take so long to adapt to the changes encountered on entry to school, particularly as, to all intents and purposes, the children are able to talk and appear to follow what is going on. Before the 1980s, teachers found that during the first half-term all the children would be able to understand what the teacher expected as well as what they didn't want to happen. The lack of development caused by the social changes described earlier in this book makes transition to school a more challenging process for all concerned.

Infant schools try to make the entry to school effortless, but it is still not easy for children who have poor communication skills. Teachers can make good use of the availability of structured support — bells rung to signal the end of an event, timetables that tell children what to do and when — all of which is more helpful to children with poor non-verbal skill development than teachers might realise. Schools have adopted many more visual prompts to help children settle, such as 'talking sticks', dolls or puppets that smile when all the children are listening, timetables written on whiteboards, and so on.

For those children who are just a little behind in their non-verbal development, this structure and routine may be sufficient to help them develop the remaining conversational skills necessary to see them through the next few years and the transition to junior school and beyond.

ENTRY TO CLASS – FIRST DAY

On the first day of term everyone may be a little nervous. But when the teacher explains the timetable — what time lunch is and what breaks are all about — your child becomes able to predict what will happen and this nervousness should start to wane. The teacher will make certain there is something to look forward to in the afternoon to help the children do the 'work' she wants them to do in the morning. You may have already had a school visit and it is also likely that you have talked through the first day with your child to help build her confidence. You will have emphasised the fact that at the end of the day you will be there to meet her and take her home.

Now all this sounds straightforward, but unpack it slightly and you will see that the whole day depends on two main non-verbal skills — interpretation and prediction. Your child needs to be able to:

- read the body language of her teachers and peers
- process all the small non-verbal clues telling her when one activity ends and another starts; this will help her anticipate any change
- know that the teacher is talking to the whole group, and that it includes her
- understand what the teacher says, even if there is no visual representation of it
- recognise that the other children are as confused as she is on this first day
- predict what behaviour the teacher expects and what will happen next
- know that what the teacher says is beneficial. She should have some non-verbal, subconscious

rule, developed over the previous four or five years, that you, as her parents, are not going to put her into harmful situations.

As long as she is able to listen and to comprehend what the teacher tells her, her life will be much easier and happier. Although there are many other possible variants, an apparently straightforward situation presents a number of challenges and your child will need to have mastered a range of non-verbal skills necessary to survive this first day, let alone the first term!

Another area of difficulty could be that it is assumed — usually because the child can talk so well — that she understands the implications of all the signs in the classroom. People have often said to me that children with the problems described here can understand all emotions. This is patently not true if you ask her the relevant questions, for example 'What is that person feeling?', 'What has made them feel that?', 'Do you ever feel like that?', 'If so, 'What makes you feel that way?' Only if a child is able to answer all these questions for all emotions, easy and complex, will you be able to say with confidence that she understands emotions.

However, children with poor non-verbal communication often understand that answering 'Yes' and smiling makes people feel happy with them and sometimes they leave them alone! Teachers who say 'She understands everything' are probably doing so on the basis that she 'sounds' as if she does because she can talk the talk. Help your child to avoid falling into this category by developing her skills to a high level before she enters school.

CONCLUSION

You should by now have a good understanding of the grounding your child needs in non-verbal communication skills. It is not so difficult to make the changes recommended in this book; at first some of the suggestions might seem strange, but like many parents before you, you will soon realise the benefits and notice a big change in your child.

You may have identified that your child is lacking some specific skills discussed here before he enters school – hopefully before he reaches the age of three – but you will certainly be able to help him by using the recommended ideas. If your child is a bit older, don't worry, you will just need to work that bit harder. Check that he is able to interpret well in all situations. If not, go back over the early stages in this book; play with him so he is encouraged to really look at faces and other non-verbal clues and make sure he can understand them.

Prevention, they say, is better than cure, so if you're a new parent you will find that the advice in this book gives your child the best possible start in avoiding difficulties later in life and adapting to the world around him.

Whatever your circumstances, once you are aware of the value of non-verbal skills you'll find that you are constantly spotting opportunities to help your child – and having fun doing so. And you will help to ensure that your child becomes a confident communicator, well equipped to get the best out of his schooling, his friendships and his family life, and to reach his full potential.

I am now a proud grandmother of a lovely little boy (ten months at the time of writing). It has been wonderful to see him develop interest in faces to the extent that he now watches who is talking and then turns to the listener to hear and see their response. His prediction skills are developing really well too. In 'Ten fat sausages' (page 52) he will turn to his grandfather who is doing the 'pops' when I say 'And one goes . . .' and before his grandad makes the 'pop'. This shows that he is picking up from the words, the intonation pattern using his previous experience and anticipating that the 'pop' is coming.

He is also starting to sign 'more' for his food and uses a range of other gestures spontaneously. He is a happy baby because he is interested in what is going on around him and things are no longer such a surprise to him.

Given the right opportunities, all children can develop these skills.

REFERENCES AND FURTHER READING

Boyce, S, *Not Just Talking: Identifying Non-verbal Communication Problems – A Life-changing Approach* (Speechmark, 2012)

Cooke, J, *Early Sensory Skills* (Speechmark, 1997)

Grobel Intrater, R, *Baby Faces series* (*Eat!/Hugs & Kisses/Peek-a-boo/Sleep/Smile/Splash*) (Scholastic Cartwheel Books, 1997–2005)

Hunt, R; Brychta, A & Schon, N, Oxford Reading Tree, *Read With Biff, Chip, and Kipper*: Level 1: Pack of 8 (Oxford University Press, 2011)

McClure, V, *Infant Massage: A Handbook for Loving Parents* (Bantam, USA, 2001)

Miller, M, *Baby Faces* (Simon & Schuster, 2009)

Palmer, S, *Toxic Childhood* (Orion Health, 2006)

Smith, C, *Let's Sign Pocket Dictionary: BSL Concise Beginner's Guide* (Co-Sign Communications, 2005)

Smith, C & Teasdale, S, *Let's Sign: Early Years*, (Co-Sign Communications, 2012) See http://www.deafsign.com/ds/index.cfm

ACKNOWLEDGEMENTS

Thank you to Dawn Terrey for the great design and Sue Gordon for her amazing editing skills, and to Stephen for being there throughout.

My thanks also go to all the children and parents who helped with photographs: Harry, Beany & Flynn; Stephen; Sophie, Lola and Asiha; Edith, Benjamin & Oliver; Isobelle & Faye; Iona.

Thank you so much, Cath Smith, for your generosity in giving me permission to use the signs you have drawn (pages 34–5, 57, 113, 127, 128, 132).

Thanks to Stokke for allowing me to use a photograph of their wonderful parent-facing buggy 'Xplory' (page 46). My grandson loves his 'Crusi', another superb Stokke buggy.

I am grateful to Shepherds Down School, Winchester, for a photograph of their symbol timetable (page 134).

The cover photograph was supplied by Getty Images.
Images on the following pages were supplied by iStock: 2, 6 (all), 7 (all), 8 (all), 9 (all), 10–11, 12, 13, 14, 16, 17, 19, 20, 22, 24–5, 26, 27, 28–9, 30–1, 36–7, 38, 40, 62, 47, 50, 53, 64–5, 69, 70, 72–3, 75, 77, 78–9, 81, 84, 87, 88, 91, 95, 96–7, 98, 101, 104, 107, 112, 115, 117, 123, 124, 128–9, 130, 132–3, 136–7, 138, 142, 145, 146, 148–9, 151.

DEDICATION
For all my grandchildren — those present and those to come. May they all be happy and contented and learn to communicate well.

Published by Not Just Talking,
13 Lynford Way, Winchester SO22 6BW

First published in the UK in 2014
Text copyright © by Sioban Boyce

Sioban Boyce has asserted her right to be identified as author of this work in accordance with the copyright, designs and patents Act, 1988.

A CIP catalogue record for this book is available from the British Library.

ISBN 978-0-9563709-0-7

Designer Dawn Terrey
Editors Sue Gordon, Stephen Boyce

Printed and bound by Sarsen Press, 22 Hyde Street, Winchester SO23 7DR www.sarsenpress.com